Primal Branding

Create Zealots for
Your Brand, Your Company,
and Your Future

Patrick Hanlon

FREE PRESS

NEW YORK   LONDON   TORONTO   SYDNEY

FREE PRESS
A Division of Simon & Schuster, Inc.
1230 Avenue of the Americas
New York, NY 10020

FREE PRESS and colophon are trademarks of Simon & Schuster, Inc.

For information about special discounts for bulk purchases,
please contact Simon & Schuster Special Sales: 1-800-456-6798 or
business@simonandschuster.com.

Designed by Dana Sloan

Manufactured in the United States of America

10 9 8 7 6 5 4 3 2 1

Library of Congress Cataloging-in-Publication Data

Hanlon, Patrick.
Primal branding: create zealots for your brand, your company, and your
future / Patrick Hanlon.
 p. cm.
Includes bibliographical references and index.
1. Brand name products. 2. Brand name products—Marketing.
3. Consumer behavior. I. Title.
HD69.B7 H3485 2006
658.8'27—dc22
                                                    2005044708

ISBN-13: 978-0-7432-7797-6
ISBN-10:   0-7432-7797-X

This book is dedicated to all my girls

Contents

PrePrimal   xi

Part One: **Going Primal**

    Introduction   3

  1. The Primal Code   9

    The Creation Story   10

    The Creed   20

    The Icons   26

    The Rituals   52

    The Pagans, or Nonbelievers   70

    The Sacred Words   72

    The Leader   78

  2. Primal Belonging   87

Part Two: **Primal Perfect**

  3. The Primal Product or Service   99

  4. The Primal Destination   159

  5. The Primal Personality   185

Part Three: **The Final Step**

6. Primal Reengineering   209

7. The Bones   233

Acknowledgments   245

Bibliography   247

Index   249

About the Author   257

Primal Branding

PrePrimal

I am sitting in a meeting at one of the largest corporations in the world. Outside the window, spring flowers bloom between empty shade trees. Returning geese fly in a scattered V shape through a crisp sky. Groundskeepers rake away leaves left from winter. And, in the conference room where I am sitting, grown men are sweating.

Once again, millions of dollars have been spent on advertising and marketing support, trying to leverage their brand. Once again, the results were less than they had promised management. Worse, the results were less than they had promised themselves.

The executive vice president in charge repeats his question. Eyes dart back and forth around the room. The executive vice president clears his throat.

"So what do you guys think? How can we become a great brand, like Nike, Apple, or Coke. Do we even think we know the answer?"

"Product innovation," someone finally pipes up.

"Let's get a great Super Bowl spot," says another.

"Create customer affinity programs," someone else jumps in.

"Yeah, relationship marketing."

"Consumer intimacy."

The executive glares. "Well, which is it?" he asks simply. Heads swivel around the table.

"Can anyone explain Google to me?" he asks. "Everyone knows them, everyone uses them, and they don't seem to advertise at all."

Someone shrugs. No one has the answer. The sad hammer of truth is that this isn't just one meeting. The meeting could have been any one of several at General Motors, Sears, IBM, or Unilever. Everywhere, smart marketers are spending millions of dollars trying to find the sticky soft tissue that attaches consumers to brands. It is characteristic that no matter who the advertiser is, once the advertising flight is over, awareness figures sag.

The paradox is that people are zealous about some brands, whether they are advertised or not. You can point to any category and see where companies have introduced innovative products that were given their introductory advertising budgets and their end-cap display and ultimately failed because they still didn't catch on. Success is not a mix of great product plus great advertising plus great price point plus great distribution. It's something else. But what?

I decided to find out. The result of my search led not only to a marketing solution but toward a new construct that redefines enterprise in terms of the human condition. It is a construct that elucidates the intuitive visceral connections people have to brands. Some of those brands are products and services like the much heralded Apple, Starbucks, and Nike. Others are personalities, social and political causes, and civic communities and the organizations that create them.

Many managers, from CEOs to product managers, are given the mandate of creating and supporting brands, but they are not given the tools. Professionals in the hard sciences of pricing, distribution, sales, and manufacture, when it comes to the soft sciences of human persuasion, they are usually ill equipped and/or ill trained. The result? The soft costs are inefficient brand planning and lack of creative problem solving. The hard costs are lost opportunity and lost dollars spent going down marketing rat holes. Worse, marketing is by rote.

In many ways, this is the story of people who are, despite the swirl of thousands of advertising impressions a day, able to break through, excite, and resonate in remarkable ways. Through gut feel, instinct, and prescient wisdom they have been able to connect the tendrils of emotion to make the difference between a product, personality, or cause that no one really cares about and something that attracts people by the millions.

Today's parity world cannot afford parity thinking. It's time for us to dig out new territory. Here's the shovel.

PART ONE

Going Primal

Introduction

In the middle of an African gully a man is down on his hands and knees. Sweat stings his eyes as he stares at the ground, not quite believing what is in front of him. He gently scrapes at the dirt, shaving away another peel of earth, revealing even more of what he recognizes as a proximal ulna, the forearm bone of a rare hominid. Paleontologist Donald Johanson spent the morning of November 24, 1974, slowly uncovering a 3.5-million-year-old skeleton. That night, Johanson and his team celebrated the discovery in their tents as the Beatles' "Lucy in the Sky with Diamonds" played in the background. Nobody remembers how, but the nickname Lucy was given to the female hominid. Lucy's discovery was flashed around the world, and her name became a household word. Equally important hominids have been discovered before and since, yet Lucy alone retains a special place in our imaginations, because she sparkles with something that other discoveries have been without. Lucy sparkles with primal code.

Every sensible CEO, entrepreneur, and product manager wants consumers to feel the same enthusiasm for their products and services that they do. People who build cities and create movements and have new ideas want to attract people in order to create followers, supporters, advocates, and financial partners.

People point to favored brands like Coke, Google, and IBM as examples of the way to do things, and they are right. But the path to mimicry seems a dead end. Within successful enterprises, whether they are products, personalities, a political or social cause, or a civic community lurks an intangible. In fact, consumers of those products become more than just customers. They feel an almost religious zeal that consumers of brands like Lestoil, Goodrich tires, and MCI never feel.

Why?

What is the magic glue that sticks together consumers and Google, Mini Cooper, and Oprah and not others? What is it that strikes the emotional chord sustained beyond the pitchman's cry? Is it a better product? A better customer experience? Better distribution? Better pricing? Each year, millions of dollars are spent by marketers trying to touch their target consumer. They buy advertising on the TV programs people love, sponsor events like Nascar, underwrite golf and tennis tournaments and marathons that their consumers enjoy, and produce emotional advertising so that consumers will feel better about their brands. Millions more are spent throwing banner ads onto Web sites that their target market hits. More millions are spent anticipating product and service niches that consumers might flock to. Even after all that, however, the connective tissue that bonds consumers to emotionally powerful brands like Coke, Disney, Apple, Starbucks, and Nike does not form.

In fact, while it's easy to explain why Coke has achieved brand loyalty after over one hundred years of consumer advertising and marketing support, it's almost impossible to reconcile how Starbucks has achieved similar consumer loyalty in the beverage category with virtually no advertising. Why? Traditionalists might point to things like great product, great experience, great locations, and great employee training. Certainly, those are factors in the success of many companies. Yet many products with great product innovation, perfect locations, terrific customer experiences, even breakthrough advertising fail to sustain the visceral traction in the marketplace that other brands achieve.

Seattle's Best Coffee shops, for example, serve terrific coffee, debatably have an experience similar to Starbucks, and have great locations. Their name even seizes the category superlative. However, Seattle's Best Coffee does not seem to have the same attraction for consumers that Starbucks has garnered. Clearly, there is something beyond traditional marketing tools that connects loyal consumers to their most beloved brands. After years of working with brands like Absolut, General Motors, Ford Motor Company, UPS, John Deere, Lego, Disney, Unilever, BellSouth, Sara Lee, IBM, Montblanc, H&R Block, and others, I wanted to find out why. The result of my search led me not to the typical answers already found in marketing and advertising, but to something much deeper.

What is a brand, anyway? Thirty years ago, a "brand" meant more than the superficial hot-iron I.D. on cattle hide; it was a product or service that customers felt something about. Today, aspiring to the higher ladder rung, virtually every product, service, or company calls itself a brand. The new meaning transformation occurred during the great conglomerate building in the 1980s and 1990s, when companies were merging one after the other. They needed new logos, new business cards, new stationery. Branding was demoted from resonance and appeal to a corporate identity project, even though the quest to become *desired* by the consuming public was more important than ever.

In the beginning the question was, Why do some products mean something to us while other products—with essentially the same features and benefits—do not? The result of this quest led to a much larger question of how ideologies—belief systems—come to exist. In the end, the search for meaning revealed not only how products and services but also companies, personalities, movements, ideologies, and civic communities unwittingly, instinctively, and through time bring together seven definable assets that construct meaning behind the brand. Perhaps the most surprising discovery of all was that while most companies try to communicate a *single* brand message to their audiences, there are in fact *seven* brand messages that must be delivered to create preferential brand appeal.

Not one message, but seven.

Primal branding is about delivering the primal code. It is a construct of seven assets that help manage the intangibles of your brand. Those seven assets are: "the creation story"; "the creed"; "the icons"; "the rituals"; "the pagans"; "the sacred words"; and "the leader." Together, these pieces of primal code construct a belief system.

Brands are belief systems. (Note: For purposes here, the term "brand" is considered to be any product, service, personality, organization, social cause, political ideology, religion, movement, or other entity searching for popular appeal.) Once you look at a brand as a belief system, it automatically gains all the advantages that enterprise strives for: trust, vibrancy, relevance, a sense of values, community, leadership, vision, empathy, commitment, and more. With the seven pieces of primal code in place you have created a belief system and products and services that people can believe in.

Believing is belonging. When you are able to create brands that people believe in, you also create groups of people who feel that they belong. This sense of community is at the center of psychologist Abraham Maslow's famous hierarchy of human needs. Whether you belong to a Masai tribe or you're a New Yorker, whether you're a baseball nut, a computer geek, a shopaholic, a marathon runner, a foodie, tekkie, biker, trekker, or triathelete, it is an essential human truth that we all want to belong to something that is larger than ourselves. That community can surround a product or service, a personality, a social or political cause, or a civic community.

Too often, we thrust products and services onto the shelves and into the streets without imbuing them with any meaning whatsoever. Relevant differentiating benefits, unique selling propositions, and functional attributes alone do not fulfill the needs of people at large, or the needs of long-term enterprise. What we call primal branding is the ability to make people feel better about your brand than another. In today's parity world, who your customer feels better about is called "preference." And it is well understood that preference creates sales. As Hal Riney, the creative guy who created Bartles & Jaymes and Saturn advertising, once remarked, "In a parity world, my best friend wins."

The primal code presents a new possibility, because it allows you the opportunity to create a culture of belief. If you have a brand that people can believe in, you have a brand that people feel they can belong to. If they feel they can belong, then you've discovered how to create the passion for your brand that zealots feel for Nike, Starbucks, and Apple. Treat them well.

In this book, we are going to decode the seven factors that work together to create believers and, ultimately, successful brands. We will give you robust examples of how others have created individual pieces of code. And we will tell the stories of people who unwittingly and over time put the pieces of code together to create success. Finally, we'll ask you what we ask everyone: Do you want to be just another product on the shelf, or do you want to become a meaningful and desired part of the culture? If your answer is the latter, please turn the page.

1. The Primal Code

All belief systems have seven pieces of code that work together to make them believable. The more pieces, the more believable the belief system becomes. When products and services have all seven pieces of code (the creation story; the creed; the icons; the rituals; the pagans, or nonbelievers; the sacred words; and the leader), they become a meaningful part of our culture. They become the Googles and Nikes of the world. When causes have all seven pieces of code, they become the civil rights movement, the women's movement, or the global fight against AIDS. When civic communities have all seven pieces of code, they become sizzling communities like New York City and Las Vegas. When personalities have the seven pieces of code in place, they become Oprah, Andy Warhol, or U2.

Certainly there have been remarkable products in the past, worthy causes and persons with extraordinary talent. But for some reason they fell short in the public imagination. When you consider that nine out of ten new products never survive in the marketplace, you have to consider that something else is in play beyond terrific innovation, distribution, and price point.

This is no longer inexplicable. They simply did not have

the pieces of primal code. Having the primal code is why brands seize the public imagination while their competitors are relegated to second place commodities and transactions.

The following pages outline the seven pieces of primal code that *together* create a sustainable belief system that provides the unarticulated, intangible emotional glue that attracts people and helps them feel that they belong. This sense of belonging manifests itself in evangelist tribes, cults, members of political parties, product geeks and enthusiasts.

While the seven pieces of code work together, they are also important individually. We will explain the central principle of primal branding and describe the individual pieces of code. To help you create the code yourselves we have spoken with people whose work it is to create icons, rituals, and other pieces of code. We have also spoken with companies who have, through gut feel and over time, put together the pieces of code and created remarkable products, companies, and organizations. While these companies did not consciously apply the pieces of primal branding, they used their gut, instinct, and intelligence to do the smart thing in the face of competitive pressures. They did what they felt was right and their consumers responded in kind.

The Creation Story

All belief systems come with a story attached. In fact, a brand is often compared to a narrative. How we originated is the foundation of myth; it fulfills an innate human desire to understand how we came to be.

"Where are you from?" is one of the first questions we ask when we meet someone new. Whether the story is about Steve Jobs and Steve Wozniak in their parents' garage creating the first personal computers, Jeff Bezos sitting in the backseat of his car writing the business plan for amazon.com, or pharmacist Dr. John Pemberton concocting a carbonated soft drink called Coca-Cola, the ur-legends of successful companies are important to us. The story of the two college kids who created Google in their dorm room. An undaunted MBA student who, scoffed at by his marketing professor, went off to create FedEx anyway. A kid named Andy Warhola who moved from Pennsylvania to New York City and changed his name to Andy Warhol.

All of these tales tell the back story and set the stage for companies and brands that we have come to trust, respect, and believe. When Sherwood Schwartz, creator of *Gilligan's Island* and *The Brady Bunch,* was asked why his shows began with a theme song outlining the show's premise, his explanation was simple. "Because the confused do not laugh," he replied. The confused do not buy, either.

Where you come from is as important for people to know as what you believe and what your advantages are. Look at most of the successful brand marks in the world and you'll notice that the story of how they started is usually top of mind. Disney. The United States of America. AIDS. Oprah. IBM. Madonna. The Soviet Union.

You probably have at least a fractured idea of how they came to be. Sometimes the connections can be fuzzy. You might have heard of Thomas Edison, and you may know of GE, but you may not realize that Thomas Edison founded

General Electric. You may have some notion that Starbucks started in Seattle without knowing that its leader was Howard Schultz or that the original Starbucks mermaid logo had breasts.

In today's telecommunicated society, we have information shelling on a daily basis (depending on which survey you want to believe, we are bombarded with two thousand to ten thousand advertising impressions a day); we cannot be expected to remember every detail.

And yet, some poke through. The question of origin is not only important to end consumers, it is important to new and existing employees, to vendor and partner relationships, to advocates—including lenders and Wall Street—and to others you want to convert to your cause. In fact, whether you are one hundred years or one hundred days old it is crucial for everyone to have an understanding of who you are and where you come from. It is the foundation of trust. As film director Errol Morris wrote in an op-ed piece in the *New York Times,* "People think in narratives—in beginnings, middles and ends." For some products, the creation story relates to personal history. Thousands of women use Tide laundry detergent simply because "my mom used it." The same is true of Betty Crocker, Campbell's soup, and other familiar household favorites. "That's where my family always went," is what others claim about favored vacation spots in Maine, Disney World, the Catskills, and Aspen. "My grandfather wore them and my father wore them," people claim of Eddie Bauer jackets, Red Wing shoes, and other long-established products. For people living in the Minneapolis area, where Target stores have existed for fifty years, the creation story

may be "That's where my mother shopped." For New Yorkers, the Target creation story might be about the place that
sells "mass with class" Michael Graves teapots and Philippe
Starck accessories.

If you were to consider yourself a brand, you could come
up with your own personal creation story. Many products,
such as colas, kinds of music, jeans, even automobiles,
become a part of personal creation stories. Drinking Coke,
eating at McDonald's with teenage peers, listening to Styx or
Dave Matthews, baking Betty Crocker brownies, riding
horses, or driving a Ford Mustang all become a part of our
personal heritage and internalized creation story. These
brands become linked to us in essential ways that become a
part of our personal codex. They may become satirized or
sneered at by later generations—or even by our own generation (witness the Gremlin, the Ford Pinto, Queen's song
"Bohemian Rhapsody," Ozzie Osbourne—think of your
own examples), but they continue as our privatized creation
saga.

Nations have creation stories, too. The United States of
America's creation story is about founding fathers tired of
taxation without representation. The creation story for Great
Britain goes back to the days of Celtic myth and through
King Arthur and Plantagenets to Prince Charles. The creation story for the Republic of China also extends back into
prehistory, to a time before the Ming emperors. India's modern creation story begins with Mohandas Gandhi and the
country's break from Great Britain, although its true creation goes back thousands of years before Christ.

Creation stories usually embody the who and the why.

Who the founder of any nation or organization was and why they started is important for people to know. It is the beginning of understanding. It is a first step to believing and belonging. Look in the magazines. Every public relations story about a new company or a new star begins with the story of who they were and where they came from. Ask almost anyone under the age of twenty and they'll tell you that Britney Spears is from New Orleans, Jessica Simpson is from Texas. Almost anyone over the age of forty knows that the Beatles were from Liverpool and Elvis Presley was a truck driver from Mississippi. Ask any golf enthusiast how Tiger Woods got his start, or any basketball fan about where Michael Jordan spent his rookie years. Ask a film buff about the origins of Stephen Spielberg or a Nascar fan about Richard Petty's first races. The creation story is the elemental foundation of a belief system. You can't ask someone to believe in something that didn't start somewhere. The question "Where's that from?" needs to be answered. Without an answer, people lose interest and turn away.

Consider the theory of evolution. The story makes sense because we know the back story of how Charles Darwin sailed on the H.M.S. *Beagle* and witnessed the strange creatures on the Galapagos Islands. The fact that we knew that he *actually saw* the creatures in order to come up with his theory makes his theory more *believable*.

Every *thing*, every *one* started somewhere.

It is late at night and I am in a limousine on my way home from a late night working with a client at his Manhattan office. Riding in a limousine may sound luxurious and elite to people who live outside of New York. In reality, it is a Lincoln Towncar that smells like air freshener if you're lucky, body sweat and curry if you're not. Limo drivers are usually from other lands: Greece, Italy, Colombia, Russia, China, India. Some of the drivers did not learn to drive in countries with weather like freezing rain and snow, nor did their automobiles have luxuries like windshield wipers that work. So they do not always use the wipers as a matter of course, only as an expensive luxury. Wipers are the handiwork of the gods and must be used sparingly, like an invocation.

On this particular night my driver is Nigerian. He wears a dark suit like a bouncer and his face bears ritual tribal scars on his cheeks and across his forehead. It is raining as we drive up the FDR. Light bounces off the wet pavement, low-hanging clouds drape the tops of buildings. As we cross the Triborough Bridge the Manhattan skyline is resplendent. Rain drizzles. Sometimes the driver uses the windshield wipers, sometimes he does not. We must not sap the power of the windshield gods. The car wends its way through neighborhoods in the Bronx until we get back onto the Deegan Expressway.

Back at the office tower, when I walked up to the car and tapped on the window for the driver to unlock the door, I heard him listening to a tape, which he turned off as I opened the door. Because I like all kinds of music, I asked him to turn the tape back on. The cassette slides into the player with a plastic click. Suddenly the inside of the car was filled with chanting voices. The tape is homemade and the music has a seminal rawness to it; it sounds of people caught on tape when they don't expect it. I ask the driver what it is. "It is my grandfather's funeral song," he replies. "When I get home-sick, I listen." His grandfather's burial soundtrack. A solitary voice sings out in a language that I do not understand. A chorus answers. The voice sings another line, again the chorus answers. I think about the people whose voices are on this tape, singing to me from ten thousand miles away, their bodies jumping up and down, their lances clacking in rhythm, their voices stolen from them and transplanted into this limousine.

"Was your grandfather a great man?" I ask the driver. "No," he says, shaking his head. "He was only a great man to me." The night is cold and wet. Rain splashes against the window glass, distorting the outside world. Neon signs advertise hamburgers and carpet and airline discounts and the colors melt into one another in gluey shapes. At two o'clock in the morning this place and time feel like a thousand miles from anywhere. The driver's personal creation story seeps into the limousine as he continues to tell me about his grandfather. A cassette tape is a small thing. You can find them beside the road almost anywhere, crushed and unspooled. All creation stories become personal. We are left to listen to them from a distance and wonder, Why did we ever leave in the first place? How do we ever get back?

The creation story often involves a mythic quest. The company's struggle to create the right product or service (the common zipper, for example, took decades—and several companies—to develop). The against-all-odds pursuit of creating the best airplane, the best running shoe, the best coffee, the best computer, the best automobile lies at the foundation of many companies (and many Hollywood screenplays). Jeff Bezos, according to press clippings, started amazon.com by writing the business plan in the backseat of his car. While Bezos wrote, his wife sat in the driver's seat and drove them to the West Coast, where Jeff presented the business plan and received funding. The creation stories of GE, Disney, and Ford Motor Company originate with the founders' personal odysseys of relentless invention. The Homeric stories of Thomas Edison, Walt Disney, and Henry Ford are part of our national psyche. And even if stories of people like Charles Goodyear, John Pemberton, and Chester Carlson are less a part of our national consciousness, they are no less important to the Goodyear, Coca-Cola, and Xerox companies.

The American Pilgrims started from Plymouth, England, and struggled to create a colony on the American shores. Nelson Mandela endured personal hardships to help found the new government of South Africa. The nations formed after the breakup of Soviet hegemony all have their own creation stories; some of them hark back to pre-Soviet times. Part of what makes a people is the story of their origin. Zionists living in Russia, Europe, and the United States sacrificed everything to return to their historic roots in the Middle East. Native American Cherokees who were transplanted to what became Indian territory in Oklahoma in the 1830s moved back to their native lands in Georgia and North Carolina. Millions of transplanted slaves returned to Africa to create the state of Liberia. Millions more American Irish have gone back to Ireland to visit their county of origin. An acquaintance used to always talk about her "cousins in Italy." At the time it seemed irrelevant (to everyone but her). Sure enough, when she had accumulated enough money she moved to Tuscany and created a bed-and-breakfast from an old mill near the family village.

Some creation stories are constructed around a vision for the future and transformation. IBM's evolution from a business supply company to a keypunch card company and ultimately into a business information and technology company is a lasting tale. The story of General Motors—the amalgamation of several automobile manufacturing companies into a single one under William C. "Billy" Durant—is another. UPS, the largest shipping and logistics corporation in the world, started as a bike messenger company.

In a world filled with conglomerate companies overseeing a portfolio of many products and services, there is a question about which entity is responsible for the creation story. Is Procter and Gamble responsible for Tide's creation story, or is Tide? Is Diageo LLC responsible for its Captain Morgan's Rum and other subsidiaries? Is Virgin responsible for its cola, airline, and wireless companies? Are General Motors and General Mills responsible for their dozens of brand names? The answer is that the product is the brand; product executives have responsibility. Clearly, the creation story for Jaguar, which is owned by Ford Motor Company, is different from the one for Ford trucks. The story for Cadillac is different from Chevrolet's, even if both are owned by General Motors. The creation story for Wheaties is different than the one for Hamburger Helper, though both are owned by General Mills.

An important point: Often, for reasons of their own choosing, some holding companies prefer to remain remote and anonymous. However, if the holding company wants to resonate with consumers and investors as well, then they should communicate their own creation story (and the other pieces of primal code) to employees, the public, investors, vendors, government, and key constituents. Part of the reason that companies like Diageo, Altria, AOL Time Warner, and others do not resonate is that, while we can comprehend the marketplace advantages, they have never adequately explained why they exist. Because we do not understand, those companies lack meaning. One conglomerate company that tried to resonate and failed a decade ago was Beatrice Foods. Their failure was not because they tried, but because they did not know how to use the elements of the primal code, beginning with a creation story. Sticking to traditional advertising and spending millions of advertising dollars propelling its product line and logo sting, the viewer still had no clear idea of Beatrice or its purpose. More important, we did not care.

The creation story is the crucial first step in providing answers to why people should care about you, or your product or service. The creation story not only answers who you are and where you come from, but helps set up the further pieces of primal code (creed, icons, rituals, pagans, sacred words, and leader). Every company was started somewhere, somehow, by someone. Like telling a good tale, the opportunity is how to make it interesting. Then you must decide where to communicate it. Do you include it in public relation efforts, on the Internet, in advertising, on packaging?

Obviously, if your company got its start making slide rules and is now making pool cues, the beginning of one does not beget the other. The story does, however, provide context. The company was successful at making slide rules, but the market for slide rules evaporated. No wonder they are also successful at making pool cues. International Business Machines was a successful purveyor of office equipment. When times changed and the marketplace evolved, they became successful providing e-business.

Elsewhere in this book you will find dozens of creation stories, all stories of modest beginnings and incredible dreams. A creation story is not a strategy. The creation story provides context; it provides meaning. It answers the question, Where did you come from? It is not about the way things are done, or the company's mission or future opportunities. Those assets are embedded in other places within the primal code.

The Creed

All ideologies begin with a set of core principles. A mission statement that declares a belief in life after death. A belief that the state is supreme. Or, if you live in Chicago, an unfortunate belief in the Chicago Cubs.

What you believe in, what you want others to believe about you, what the mission is, are not easy statements to make. Imagine the United States of America brand without its Declaration of Independence, its Bill of Rights, or the Pledge of Allegiance. Google provides unbiased, accurate, and free information to the public. The world ecology movement's creed is to save the planet (and ourselves).

Corporate America understands the value of spending time trying to fashion the word set that defines a company's mission. Defining, understanding, and communicating your mission are critical to the success of your brand, both internally and externally. Confused employees and coworkers cannot motivate and persuade others. Confused prospects do not buy; undirected managers wither, shrug their shoulders, and move on. Creeds differentiate and motivate. To borrow film director Sidney Pollack's metaphor, the creed is the spine that supports the entire enterprise. Note the resonance of some of the best:

> *All men are created equal.*
> *Blacks are equal to whites.*
> *Women are equal to men.*
> *Peace on Earth.*
> *Save the whales.*
> *It's the real thing.*

These are all simple, concise statements that embody hugely bold ideas. The creed is the singular notion that you want people to believe. Sometimes that notion may be part of your corporate mission; sometimes your mission must enfold other concepts in order to satisfy business concerns. Imagine that the creed is a simple, bold statement that you could put on a placard. Sometimes the creed is simply the boiled-down expression that is communicated in your advertising: "Think different." "Just do it." "Soup is good food." These may not be the corporate mission statements for Apple, Nike, or Campbell's, but they certainly communicate what you should believe about those products. Clearly, if you are Ford Motor Company, the creed for Jaguar and the creed for the F-350 pickup trucks are going to be remarkably different, just as their creation stories are different.

Many companies are founded by outstanding personalities of dynamic talent, resources, and imagination: Richard Branson, Bill Gates, Ted Turner, David Ogilvy, Henry Ford, Tom Watkins, Steve Jobs. When these people retire and move on, their visions become a series of anecdotes and quoted remarks from those who worked at their side. For the next generation the founder's legacy becomes a text of quotes. Step-by-step, whether due to interpretation, changing times, or changes in philosophy, their critical vision erodes and dissipates.

This is why companies falter when the founder steps out. Witness Apple after Steve Jobs left in the 1990s. At least a part of Michael Eisner's controversial struggle at The Walt Disney Company centered on whether or not he was sustaining Walt Disney's original vision.

Not all companies are able to stick to their original creed. As time and markets change, companies must change or die. Texas Instruments and Xerox are in fundamentally different businesses today. GE has evolved from the company that Thomas Edison founded. Time, Inc., has merged, expanded, and multiplied many times beyond the magazine that Henry Luce started.

Alastair Johnston is vice chairman of IMG, the world's leading sports management agency with a client roster that includes Tiger Woods, Jack Nicklaus, Serena Williams, Derek Jeter, Jennifer Capriati, Martina Navratilova, John

McEnroe, Charles Barkley, Picabo Street, and others. "In sports, someone is always going to come along and break your record," says Johnston. "Ninety-nine percent of athletes endure as commercial properties only while they're playing."

Johnston and IMG founder Mark H. McCormack faced this challenge with golf legend Arnold Palmer. "It became clear to Mark and myself that to be perceived as a winner is very short-term," declares Johnston. "Winning is not enduring. What is enduring is success. So one of the things we tried to do was to build Palmer with being someone who is successful. Success is a lot more enduring than being a winner. Secondly, more people can relate to being successful than they can to winning." IMG worked hard to change Arnold Palmer's brand credo from "Arnold Palmer: PGA champion" to "Arnold Palmer: successful businessman."

TBWA\Chiat\Day, the advertising agency that has produced dozens of great campaigns, from the Energizer Bunny to Apple's "Think different" campaign to Absolut vodka had a simple operating creed: "How big can we get before we get bad?"

UPS had a creed in the 1980s of being "the tightest ship in the shipping business." The curious thing about this credo, also the theme of its advertising campaign, was that it was reflexive. At the time, United Parcel Service was not the tightest ship in the shipping business, but it *wanted to be*. UPS projected its vision of what it wanted to be on the airwaves, convincing prospects and employees alike.

Personal care products company Aveda has a simple creed that is the backbone of their business. The statement was written by founder Horst M. Rechelbacher:

Our mission at Aveda is to care for the world we live in, from the products we have to the ways in which we give back to society. At Aveda, we strive to set an example for environmental leadership and responsibility not just in the world of beauty, but around the world.

"It is what we guide the company by," says Chris Hacker, senior vice president of marketing and design. "It is on the wall in the lobby but, more importantly, it is in the heart of every person who works here."

At Barnes & Noble, the world's largest bookseller, founder Len Riggio reminds his people that they are not in the business of selling laundry detergent or soda water or blue jeans. They sell books. Books are filled with information, knowledge, and wisdom. Their work is not a mere over-the-counter transaction, he advises, but an ennobling enterprise. Barnes & Noble employees are reminded, "We do important work."

"There absolutely are core principles," says Opus One chief executive officer David Pearson, who decries the use of a mission statement for creating one of Napa Valley's most cherished wines. "When you're here at the winery, it doesn't really feel like a place of business. It feels like you're in the combined residences of the Mondavi and Rothschild families. There is a sense of mission about what we're doing, which is trying to produce the very highest quality wine possible from our vineyards and have what we think of as an attainable luxury available to consumers." The winery also has a missionary sense of wanting to create a legacy. American culture has a tendency to flip to the next newest, brightest, fastest thing. As a result, the great wineries of the 1970s and 1980s are considered differently these days, and America doesn't have a great winery that's lasted twenty years. "Our passion and mission right now, being twenty-five years old," says Pearson, "is to do the necessary things, the proper things, so that Opus One is still considered one of the great wines in California twenty years from now."

The creed is what you want people to believe. "All men are created equal" (so are women), is a fundamental statement about humankind that has driven the beliefs of the United States of America and the civil rights movement, and has had pervasive effects throughout the world. *Semper fi* is an assertive anthem that leads Marines to fight and die. Volvo has a creed to design and produce the world's safest automobiles. Starbucks's creed of being "the third place" (the other two being home and office) is a wholehearted credo for hospitality, the kitchen away from home, a comfortable state of mind. (And keep your senses tuned for Starbucks's *fourth* place.) The creed for the Singapore Zoo simply reads:

> *To be a world-class leisure attraction striving to provide excellent exhibits of animals displayed in their natural environments, for the purpose of recreation, education and conservation.*

If someone can write a lucid mission statement for a zoo, certainly one can be written for any intelligent enterprise.

Once you have the creed that defines who you are and why you exist, it must be integrated with the other elements of the primal code to create a holistic system of belief.

The Icons

Icons are quick concentrations of meaning that cause your brand identity and brand values to spontaneously resonate. The Nike swoosh. The Apple start-up "bong." The sound of the Pentium gliss. The smell of Cinnabons, the American flag, the Coke bottle, the Absolut bottle, the Beatles's mop hair, the rock group Kiss's make-up, the Budweiser Clyesdales, the Tide package, the national anthem. Whether the icons are visual, sound bites, smell, or some other form, they are sensory imprints that instantly summon the brand essence. And we recognize these icons early on. When my daughter Devin was just eighteen months old, she would point out the McDonald's arches from her infant seat.

The simplest and often easiest icon to recognize is the company logo. We are all familiar with the Coke red ribbon, the Starbucks mermaid, Target's red bull's-eye, as well as brand marks for the Red Cross, the Nike swoosh, and dozens more. Technically, some of those are not logos at all, but word marks. "FedEx technically doesn't have an icon, it has a word mark," explains Susan Nelson, executive director of strategy at Landor. The international design firm designed the word mark for FedEx, as well as logos for H & R Block and BP. (The next time you look at the FedEx logo, be sure to spot the arrows inside.) People in the public eye can also become icons for their brand. Richard Branson has become synonymous with everything Virgin. Mick Jagger and Keith Richards are icons for the Rolling Stones. Michael Eisner, Jack Welch, Steve Jobs, Bill Gates, and others have also become icons for the brands they stand for. So are personified icons like the Michelin man, Tony the Tiger, Betty Crocker, the Green Giant, Ronald McDonald, Mr. Clean, and others. Dr. Martin Luther King, Jr., and Nelson Mandela have become icons for civil rights. Mohandas Gandhi has become the icon for nonviolent civil disobedience. Personality brands like Andy Warhol, Madonna, Martha Stewart, Oprah, and others have become their own invaluable icons. Other personalities also have icons to distinguish them, like Stevie Wonder's sunglasses, Elvis's stage outfits, Frida Kahlo's unibrow. These icons inhabit valuable mental real estate that is immediately and indelibly attached to that ideology. Post-it Notes, the Absolut bottle, the Coke bottle, and the iPod are also iconic shapes.

There are thousands of companies in the world, and every one of them has a logo. Yet comparatively few of those logos are as iconic as those of VW, Coke, Tide, IBM, and eBay. According to Michael Bierut at Pentagram Design in New York City (the company that has designed logos for Citibank, the New York Jets, United Airlines, and others) logo icons have to be quick studies yet abstract enough that they can hold meaning that isn't necessarily there. "When a logo is unveiled for the first time, people will have a flood of associations," says Bierut. Logos communicate at some fast, prearticulate level that means nothing yet means everything. "Icons like Nike mean nothing in themselves," adds Bierut, "but they've amassed some kind of meaning in a very expensive way, I think, through everything else that becomes attached to them." That attachment, of course, is all that matters. But creating split-second resonance is not easy. Hundreds of logo designs may be created before that perfectly succinct logo is found. Or felt.

Visual icons should attract attention and assert requisite values of authority, leadership, and confidence. And they should provide relevance. It is the misguided company that lets their logo stand idle since the day it was invented. Successful companies like John Deere, 3M, UPS, and IBM have a long-standing tradition of updating and reasserting their logo mark in the face of new competition, new markets, and new leadership. Even comparative newcomer Starbucks altered its original logo (which showed a mermaid with bared breasts) when the coffee company went national.

Freeman Thomas designed the revolutionary Audi TT and was codesigner of the new VW Beetle. In the iconography of car design, the Beetle and TT are celebrated examples of fast-forward thinking. "Cars give off messages of what they are," says Thomas. "It's this way with anything. You look at a racehorse and you don't have to be an expert on racehorses to know that it's very athletic, very fast, very sporty, and it's designed to have only one person on top. Those are the messages, those are the palette."

It is the challenge and opportunity for car designers to create their own message. And whether you spot a vehicle at a car show or coming toward you at sixty miles per hour that message is interpreted in seconds. Therefore, the message must be simple. In Thomas's words, it must be "ultimate purity." While reinventing the VW Beetle, Jay Mays and Freeman Thomas were given the challenge of simplifying Erwin Komenda's already classic design. "We wanted to distill the essence of the original Beetle into a model statement," says Thomas. "If you distill Mickey Mouse, it's three circles.

The Beetle is three arcs on the side. From the top view, it's an oval with four ovals attached to it. So you keep going around and distilling this idea. I felt that Komenda was such an inspiration in the way that he approached design, that's the way I approached it."

Legend has it that Thomas sketched the VW redesign on a cocktail napkin. He admits that the textures of hotel stationery, beer mats, and other found writing surfaces can be inspirational. "Culture really inspires me," he says. "The different people, the buildings, the landscape, the smell. That to me is the ultimate inspiration. Being in a magical place, an iconic place." Being in the Porsche design studio for seven years was also an inspiration. "They were absolute mentors to me in building up a design and working within that philosophy," says Thomas.

Since it had never existed before, the Audi TT was a design challenge of an entirely different sort. Bereft of the laudable design history of Porsche or VW, the Audi brand was a complex mix of styles. "Audi was so complicated, I took it as kind of a challenge," says Freeman Thomas. He tried to edit the form into a shape that communicated the essence of Audi design and technology. "When you look at the car from the side and you see that line that connects between the wheel wells, that to me was the communication of Quattro," says Thomas. "It was a perfect way to take the soft shape and create a very technical facet to it and to really emphasize the wheel flares." He also used that technical line to connect the lighting systems. The face of the car is very emotional, more Audi Union–like. "There's a lot of Porsche 356 and 550 Spyder," declares Thomas. There were other inspirations for the Audi TT, like the Porsche 550 LeMans Coupe.

While slightly off point, no car buff can walk away from a guy like Freeman Thomas without asking which cars are his favorites. "The Jag XJ13. I'm absolutely in love with that car," he responds. "I think the Ferrari P4s and P3s are just amazing. The Porsche 917." And what cars does he own himself? "I have some old Porsche 356s," he says. "And I have a 1969 Ferrari Dino and I have a Porsche 911 that I'm in love with. But I like it all." You get the sense from this incredible designer that these icons not only shaped his affection for the Porsche, Ferrari, and Jaguar brands, but ultimately our loves of the VW Beetle and Audi TT.

On Aisle 7 in the local grocery store stands a rack of extraordinary kitchen tools. The white plastic utensils include potato mashers, can openers, bread knives, cheese planes, and garlic presses. Instead of metal or wood, the handles are plastic and oversized, designed to fit better in the hands of older persons plagued with arthritis.

You may have already heard the OXO story. Sam Farber, a retired Costco executive, heard his wife, Betsey, complain how her arthritis made it difficult to grip kitchen utensils. After some research and product testing, Farber came out with the OXO Good Grips product line in 1990. The oversized handles with stylish black ribbing quickly attracted the American eye. And just as the silhouettes of the Coke bottle and the Volkswagen Beetle became iconic for thirst quenching and fun driving, OXO tools became iconic for ease of use and utility. "The handle becomes the tangible element that burns an image in the consumer's mind," says Davin Stowell of Smart Design, the firm that designed OXO tools. "The good experience is the core of the memory. The shape or the black rubber may be the visual memory."

OXO went through several product iterations before they came up with their famous iconic handle. "We spent a lot of time creating the icon," explains Stowell. "If you watch somebody pick it up for the first time, you'll notice the first thing is, they make a visual connection with those fins. As soon as they pick it up, their fingers go on them and they start playing with them, squeezing them. Once they've done that, the whole concept has been communicated to them. It attracts them from a distance, they see something different, their hand goes to it, and they make that instant identification with it. And that's exactly what you want them to know about it—it's a great handle, a great tool."

Fender guitar shapes like the famed Telecaster and Stratocaster are also iconic. (So are the shapes of the Gibson V-Factor ["Flying V"] and Les Paul, the Gibson Jumbo 200 and the Martin D-18.) The Mini Cooper automobile is iconic as a road rally vehicle. The John Deere tractor is iconic of our agrarian past. The fins on a 1957 Cadillac are iconic. The *Mona Lisa* by Leonardo da Vinci and *David* by Michelangelo are icons of the Renaissance. The Christmas tree shape and smell is an icon of Christmas, as is Santa Claus. You need only be reminded that Santa Claus is a relatively new invention (only one hundred years old) to understand that icons can be layered one over the other, providing a richer and more resonant belief system.

Each year, new color swatches are published for graphic

artists and fashion designers. This fresh palette provides the iconic color recommendations of the new season.

Architect Richard Meier is famous for his iconic use of the color white. So great is his white reputation that, after Meier was selected as architect for the $1 billion Getty Center, in a fit of pique the local homeowner's association wrote stipulations that buildings at the new site could not be white. (Instead, the Getty is predominantly an off-white travertine quarried from a site near Rome.) When asked how he feels about the color, Meier smiles. "I'm happy with it." His signature white is more than idiosyncrasy. In his acceptance of the Pritzker Prize, Meier explained that white reflects and amplifies perception of the world around it. "It is against a white surface that one best appreciates the play of light and shadow, solids and voids," he declared.

Packaging can also be iconic. Ask anyone who collects Wheaties boxes, Beatles albums, or Barbie dolls. Those who manufacture and market DVDs, CD-ROMs, and other software understand that while the disk is elemental, it's the box that surrounds the disk that supplies on-shelf sizzle. Packaging for the iPod U2 Special Edition 20GB was a square cube many times the dimension of the iPod it held—and sold for fifty dollars more.

There's packaging on people, too. Wigs as seen on British lords are icons of Georgian England (and British courts). Neck collars as seen in portraits of Queen Elizabeth and Sir Walter Raleigh are icons of another era. More recently, the Armani suit is iconic of a certain lifestyle, as are mod, goth, surfer, and skater clothing styles. Tattoos are the icons of a racy subculture. Cowboy hats are icons of the American West and country western music. Lederhosen is an icon of the European Alps (and slapstick humor). And the wedding dress is an icon of the marriage ceremony.

Reem Acra is a fashion designer who has designed wedding gowns for Christina Applegate and Melissa Joan Hart (and gowns for starry-night red carpet appearances for Jennifer Lopez, Reese Witherspoon, Halle Berry and Lisa Kudrow). "I am not just designing dresses," declares Acra. "I am designing *a moment.*" In a symbolic ceremony such as a wedding, the dress becomes metaphor. Says Acra, "In the wedding, the bride is changing her life. She has that one opportunity to say something visually, who she is, who she wants to be, her inner self. And it's very expressive in the wedding gown."

This figures in the design of the dress, where meaning is crucial. "Pure and virginal might be more or less embellished, more atonal, the embroidery would be the color of the fabric," explains Acra. "The veil would be more covered, longer, and the front would be to the floor.

"Sexy would be push-up under the bust, it would have cleavage, tighter at hip level. Believe me, a quarter of an inch makes a difference between being sexy or not sexy."

Reem Acra names her dresses accordingly, with signature titles like Glisten, Unforgettable, Princess, Good Luck, Bikini (yes, a bikini wedding gown), Contessa, Lady, Fantasy, and Gypsy.

That "bam!" moment when the bride appears at the start of the wedding aisle or when the starlet emerges from the limousine happens in a blink. "That's the reason I make my dresses over the top," explains Acra. "It's not about making just a pretty dress, it's about making an expression." She pauses. "The feeling that one has is so extraordinary. I think that's why it becomes iconic at the same time. It's all related to feeling."

There is no jewel quite as iconic as a diamond. Rose diamonds, briolette diamonds. Full cut, fancy shaped, and colored, diamonds are Manhattan jeweler Fred Leighton's best friend. Fred Leighton Ltd. decks out the stars on Oscar night with fabulous antique diamonds restaged in fabulous contemporary designs. "We take old jewelry and reconfigure it to make it happy for today," smiles Leighton, who festoons stars like Uma Thurman, Natalie Portman, and Scarlett Johansson with his diamond hairpins, earrings, broaches, and necklaces.

Walking the red carpet wearing a Fred Leighton creation is not just showbiz, it's big business for Leighton. "You get somebody who's beautiful and elegant and knows how to show it off, it's different than getting a model to work the jewelry," says Leighton. "When someone like Sophia wants to show it, she has that magic that makes people all over the world call us." When Sarah Jessica Parker wears her Fred Leighton earrings, people call the next day asking to buy "Sarah's earrings." Nicole Kidman wore Leighton's India earrings and he sold over fifty pairs.

How these diamond confections are created is part arcane art form, part wizardry. An example: "You don't sell many tiaras," says Leighton. "We had a gorgeous one that we sold to Mrs. Prada. We turned it upside down and made sort of a cap out of it instead of it being a tiara. She saw it and put it on and had to have it. Because it was just something great and different looking and wonderful."

Looking wonderful is not always easy, even for the lushly gorgeous. Leighton works with star designers and stylists as he tries to turn accessories into necessities. How, for example, does one design something for J. Lo if she's wearing a one-shoulder Valentino, as she did at a recent Oscar ceremony? "You have to do something that fits the form of her face and the length of her neck and where the dress starts," Leighton explains. "If you want to have a long pair of earrings, you have to make sure she's wearing the type of dress where the movement of the dress won't interfere with the earrings. The earrings were three-and-a-half or four inches long. It's normally not a thing that we would send her, yet for this dress they were absolutely perfect."

Fred Leighton is a natural at placing an iconic stone upon a Hollywood icon. He placed a 50-carat diamond in an eye-catching spot on Catherine Zeta-Jones when she was pregnant. "She had this thing just hanging in her cleavage which was nice and busty. It was fantastic," grins Leighton. "This 50-carat rock." He throws up his hands and shrugs. "When you get somebody wearing the right thing, it's the right thing."

An icon can also take on social significance, like the yellow ribbon. With origins dating back to the American Civil War, the yellow-ribbon-folded-on-itself icon gained contemporary notice when it became the theme of a Tony Orlando and Dawn song in 1973. The song was resurrected in 1980 when Iranians took fifty-two Americans hostage in Iran during the Carter administration. The design of the yellow ribbon turned up again in the mid-1980s as a red ribbon showing support for AIDS victims. As a passive-aggressive show of support for AIDS victims, the icon has been effectively translated into a number of colors: pink for breast cancer, green for Lyme disease and the environment, and most recently red, white, and blue or Stars and Stripes with words for those who still don't get it: God Bless America and Support Our Troops fighting in Iraq.

"The ribbon somehow has come to suggest this peculiar statement that's neither pro or con," says Michael Bierut of Pentagram. "It has this limp-noodle quality that's not strident and doesn't seem as belligerent as an eagle with claws and arrows."

Both Nike and the Lance Armstrong Foundation (LAF) point to no one person as the originator of the popular LIVE-STRONG yellow wristband. "Basically the idea came from our partners at Nike, who had been marketing colored wristbands for various sports teams," says Tiffany Galligan, associate director of the Lance Armstrong Foundation.

As Lance Armstrong's licensor Nike was looking for ways to work with the Lance Armstrong Foundation, and the foundation was looking for ways to work with Nike. The idea Nike put on the table was a simple yellow wristband. "Initially, the band was going to have the words 'carpe diem' on it," informs Galligan. Dodging that cliché, Nike came across the word marriage LIVESTRONG, which had been created by an Austin, Texas, agency for the foundation's education campaign. "Luckily, they loved the name LIVESTRONG," laughs Galligan.

The loopy band of yellow plastic was launched for the 2004 Tour de France. The yellow matches the color of the Tour de France winner's jersey, and is also symbolic of cancer survivors. "We heard stories about people wearing yellow shirts or yellow hats during chemotherapy," says Bianca Elise Bellavia, director of communications at LAF. The powerful image of Lance Armstrong cancer survivor, wearing the Tour de France victory yellow, was an emotionally mind-blowing image. Reinforced by heavy promotion from Nike, the iconic yellow "baller bands" sold for one dollar at sporting goods stores and other outlets all over the United States. "Cancer is an issue that is pervasive, and we gave people something to do about it for one dollar," says Bellavia. Within a year after its introduction over 42 million wristbands had been sold, making it one of the most successful cause-related marketing efforts ever.

Since 1876, the year that General George A. Custer fought at Little Big Horn, the iconic Heinz ketchup bottle has been an almost obligatory part of the American table. With an overwhelming market share, the Heinz bottle has become ubiquitous at virtually every grocery store in the country. In 1999, faced with generic store brands and staunch competitor Hunt's, Heinz managers wanted to do something to reexcite their consumers and maintain leadership.

"You'll see a lot of marketing in-shelf these days," says Robin Teets, senior manager of marketing PR at Heinz consumer products U.S.A., in Pittsburgh, Pennsylvania. "You'll see end-cap displays, neck hangers, and little 'take one' coupons and stuff like that. But at the time that we started this, no one had ever really used the label in quite the way that we were thinking." Working with their advertising agency, Leo Burnett in Chicago, Heinz managers turned bravely to the product label itself. How could they change the icon without changing the icon? "Consumers already think of Heinz ketchup as an iconic brand," explains Teets. "We thought, Wouldn't it be great to think of fun things on-shelf, in place of what it normally says, which is 'Heinz Ketchup.'" With messages like "14 billion French fries can't be wrong." "Sunscreen for French fries," "Quiet, please. Tomatoes meeting inside," and "Not new and improved," Heinz reenergized their icon.

"We received tremendous positive response by doing this," claims Teets. When 95 percent of Americans have ketchup in their cupboard at any given moment, having fun with their one-hundred-year-old icon created a new way to engage consumers in a way that they were not typically engaged. "We need to remind them why they love it," says Teets, "and keep people talking about ketchup." So far, they only talk about Heinz.

The iconic yellow frame of *National Geographic* magazine (which first appeared in 1910) surrounds the cover photo, inviting people to look inside. *National Geographic*'s most iconic cover—although it seems presumptuous to choose just one—is the beatific gaze of Sharbat Gula, the teenage Afghan girl who stared at us from the June 1985 issue. According to *National Geographic,* Sharbat's tourmaline-eyed unwavering stare is the most recognized photograph in the magazine's history. But the thousands of other images in the magazine are also valuable icons. Each month, the appearance of colorful tree frogs, full-breasted natives, undersea exploration, bursting volcanoes, and toothsome dinosaurs have been welcome sights for thousands of subscribers, from Emperor Haile Selassie, Theodore Roosevelt, and Al Capone to your local public library.

Sound can also be used to summon feelings for a brand. The *Tonight Show* theme song and "The Star-Spangled Banner" are all examples of sound icons that make us think instantly of valuable brands. The ambulance siren and fire alarm are iconic sounds of emergency. Music is a powerful icon that marches us to war and marches us to the wedding altar. Music helps us drive to work in the morning and helps us woo one another ("that's our song"). It is common wisdom in the movie industry that 50 percent of a film is music. The *Jaws* theme is iconic. So is Hitchcock's oft-imitated *shreek! shreek! shreek!* from the *Psycho* shower scene. Western themes from the movie *Rio Grande* and the Marlboro Man commercials. For years, the themes of Ennio Morricone have been iconic soundscapes connected with spaghetti westerns like *A Fistful of Dollars*. The "Intel inside" musical signature featured at the end of virtually every computer television commercial is one of the most ubiquitous music icons ever, heard about every five minutes somewhere in the world. (The reason being that Intel pays a portion of advertising dollars to any computer company that uses the Intel musical signature in their commercials.) The single-note Apple start-up bong is also iconic. So are the chimes that signal the end of intermission at the New York City Metropolitan Opera.

Teaching theory shows that information that has a melody to it attaches itself to memory more readily than spoken information. (Remember singing your ABCs? And be aware that the Burger King's "have it your way" jingle hasn't been on-air for twenty years.)

Thad Spencer, CEO of Asche and Spencer Music, creates music for Nike, Ikea, MTV, and Budweiser as well as arranges music scores for films like *Monster's Ball.* "When you're writing music, there are ups and downs, points of happiness and sadness, tension and release. Those are the emotions that you are manipulating throughout the course of a feature film," says Spencer. There are tried-and-true methods of musically signaling a chase scene, a love scene, a battle, a product introduction. "The trick," says Spencer, "is to do those same things but in a much more subtle way. To not use the standard melodic tools and come at it from a behind-the-scenes approach, so when the music is present it seeps into your experience, and you're not even knowing that it happened." Silence is also golden. "I'm more inclined to have less music than more," says Spencer. "Because when the music enters it has so much more power." Sound, like the sense of smell, has a connection to deep subliminal emotions. "It's a real mystery why we have such an emotional attachment to the arrangement of twelve tones," says Spencer. "It never fails to amaze or intrigue me."

An interesting note on iconic music is that Aeon Flux, the animated icon that came out of MTV's Liquid Television series and created by mad genius Peter Chung, was originally conceived to mess with the conventions of traditional scoring, reports director Robin Steele. Whenever Aeon is doing something nasty and homicidal—some scenes are bloodbaths—the music score is upbeat, pleasant, and reassuring. Conversely, when there's a moment you think should be appealing—a romantic scene or such—the music goes dark and demented. It's an interesting, extremely narrow concept that became such a subliminally disturbing phenomenon that it could not help but attract notice and appeal. Watch for the movie.

White picket fences are the romanticized icon for relaxed, small-town living. Pillars signal authority and state. Booksellers like Barnes & Noble and Borders fill their retail space with iconic comfy leather chairs and sofas, translating the French literary salon for strip-mall America. The comfy library aesthetic has helped them become de facto community literary centers. "In some of the towns we are located in across the country," says a Barnes & Noble executive, "people would never find themselves engaged in a book or in reading if it weren't for the fact that we were there."

Taste is also an icon. The sweet, carbonated tickle of Coke. The taste of Krispy Kreme donuts. Oreos. McDonald's french fries. Snaps licorice. A & W root beer. Wheaties. These are all iconic taste sensations that resonate with meaning. Through released protons, ion channels, and G-protein-coupled receptors channeled to the brain, we are rewarded with the sensations of salty, sour, sweet, bitter, and umami (a meaty, savory taste produced by several amino acids and nucleotides; think MSG). Up to a hundred cells reside on each taste bud, each one able to sense all the tastes. In other words, your tongue is not divided into Balkan states of sweet, sour, or bitter. Negotiating these sensations is the work of research kitchens located in food corporations around the world.

"I was inspired by the taquerias in San Francisco," says

Steve Ells, chief executive officer of Chipotle Mexican Grill (that's pronounced Chi-POHT-lay). "I was intrigued by the packaging—that giant flour tortilla with everything on the inside. I thought, Wow, I could have similar ingredients sexed up a bit and made lighter and seasoned in a way that made them a little more forward than typical Mexican food." Chipotle (its name comes from the ripened jalapeño pepper that has been smoked and dried) has reexcited a fast-food category that seemed as dead as the Frito bandito. Started in 1993 with a single store next to the University of Denver campus, Chipotle now has over four hundred restaurants around the country and is over 90 percent owned—but not managed— by McDonald's. Unlike the burger chain, Chipotle isn't about consumer focus groups, food panels, and people in test kitchens. "That's me," laughs Steve Ells. "There is no *people*."

A former chef, Ells got his experience in San Francisco, where his influences were stars de cuisine Jeremiah Towers and Alice Waters. "I started Chipotle with the idea to create an experience that's fast and not fast food," Steve Ells explains. And while Chipotle Mexican Grill sounds like it might be an upscale Taco Bell, Ells demurs. "I don't even think of Chipotle as a Mexican restaurant. We have tacos and burritos and things that sound Mexican, but to me it's about great-tasting food served in an atmosphere sympathetic to the food, prepared freshly, and served to the customer in a way that's customizable." He adds, "Quickly."

It's not about having heat and spice, it's about taste. Some things at Chipotle do have heat and spice (it's an option), but it's more about having depth and character and layering flavors together. "I use a lot of citrus for seasoning," says Ells.

"There's lemon or lime juice in just about everything. And that balances with salt very nicely. Things like toasted cumin seeds for the beans. The use of fresh herbs like oregano and cilantro." Chipotle also uses pork, chicken, and beef that are raised naturally, without hormones and antibiotics.

Freshness has been important since the beginning. "When I started, the very first day, with just one restaurant we used to pick oregano off the stems and chop them," declares Ells. "We still do that today." Many chains add items to the menu as a way of continuing to draw customers. So far, Ells has not. He introduced a dish called Bol a few years ago, which presented ingredients without the tortilla wrap. Last year, he introduced en SALADa. "Big pieces of romaine lettuce that normally we shred for tacos," says Ells, plus the other ingredients usually wrapped in a tortilla. The news with the salad is its Chipotle-Honey vinaigrette. Red wine vinegar, chipotle, honey, fresh oregano, salt and pepper, and oil. "That vinaigrette really brings out some different flavors, so it's a completely different experience," attests Ells. And in today's world of multimillion-dollar kitchens and consumer tests, how did Chef Ells create it? "I just went over to the store and made up a vinaigrette."

For twelve years, Chipotle has grown thanks to new markets, endless expansion, and a fresh idea. With American families working hard, moving fast, and not always having enough time to sit down to dinner, Steve Ells says he wanted to develop an experience that nourished the soul as well as the body. Only time will tell if better tasting food from Chipotle will help us get there. Steve Ells adds that he started Chipotle because he wanted to create a cash cow that would help finance a real restaurant. "I now realize that Chipotle *is* a real restaurant," he smiles.

In a little workroom in Kirkham, England, Frank Knight works on the proper aroma for what the streets of Glasgow, Scotland, might have smelled like in the 1930s. "Obviously there would be rubbish in the streets, some horse manure, and the smell of coal," says Knight. He allows that there's a lot of personal interpretation involved. On this particular project the client is insisting that Knight has more work to do. "It's really hard to explain aroma," says Knight. "Sometimes they may say it wants a bit more coal, or a bit more this or that. It's a little bit of interpretation."

Knight is owner of Dale Air Limited, a company that delivers aroma solutions. Much of their work is for museums and for point of sale. Their projects have included creating the smells of Antarctic explorer Captain Robert Scott's hut, Vikings, dinosaurs, even flatulence. "We had two inquiries in a week for that," laughs Knight. One was for an exhibit at the Imperial War Museum on World War I trench warfare; the second came from a toilet manufacturer. Knight points out that smell is an important part of education. In most museums today you can touch and see and listen. It's just as important to smell. The paleontologists at London's Natural History Museum agreed. For their *Tyrannosaurus rex* exhibit they asked Knight what a *T. rex* smelled like? "Not nice," answers Knight. "The teeth were spread apart, so there was rotten meat between them. They would have had sores from fighting. Some of the meat wouldn't have been fresh (if they bumped into something dead on the trail, it was a free meal).

So that wouldn't have smelled good either." It took a few attempts to get it right. "We were going to do its breath," says Knight. "But they said, We've had second thoughts. It would have driven people out of the museum." Finally, they agreed on an aroma that included part dinosaur breath, part swampy surroundings.

But it's not all flatulence and dinosaur breath. Knight is included in a branding effort for a travel agency, which includes scents of coconut tanning oil and seashore. He created the myriad aromas of an Egyptian spice market for a 3D virtual holiday. And in nursing homes they blow in memory scents for the aged.

"The smell of a coal fire and Monday wash day laundry soap can bring many memories back," says Knight about the nursing home project. Fragrances of the past stir memories and reduce the effects of loneliness and old age. "The smell gets old people talking, the thoughts come back, and they talk to each other," says Knight. "It works well, we think."

In an attempt to combine scent and the digital age, Knight is working with another company that has identified a dozen basic smells. With a plan that reeks faintly of 1950s Smell-a-Vision, they intend to partner with a film company to introduce the sense of smell to movie theaters. Imagine the smell of cordite during a war battle scene, the aroma of a witch's brew during one of Harry Potter's magic potion classes, the smell of lavender as lovers walk through a field.

Another thought. "People have corporate logos and corporate design and appearances; we think companies should have a corporate aroma. If you go into a bank and they have an aroma there, it will remind you of that bank."

*   *   *

At least one company agrees. When guests walk into any one of the over seven thousand Aveda salons around the world, they are greeted with a signature Aveda aroma. "The primary Aveda aroma that you'd notice is Shampure," says Chris Hacker, senior vice president of marketing and design. "It has a denseness and richness that people recognize immediately." In herbal terms, Shampure's aroma is an alchemy of lavender, rosemary, and grapefruit. Aveda makes certain that its aromas are distinct. Aveda's Chakra II: Attraction lotion, for example, has forty-four pure flower and plant essences.

"We focus on essential oils, which are distilled from plants, which we sometimes call the 'spirit' of the plant," says Peter Matravers, vice president in charge of research and development. "We want to do more natural discovery than invention." While other research houses seek new scents according to consumer preference studies, Aveda scientists are charged with the dual purpose of not only finding new aromas, but also studying their therapeutic properties. While the therapeutic properties of lavender, chamomile, mint, and rose have already been well documented, Matraver's new charge is to find the therapeutic value hidden in specimens of guava, babassu, and ylang ylang.

"Of course, we also need to do consumer preference," says Peter Matravers, "but that would be done in parallel with therapeutic responses." Aveda has a partnership with the University of St. Petersburg in Russia to determine clinical responses to aromas (curiously, the University of St. Petersburg is where Ivan Pavlov conducted his famous dog experiments). "The route of how the limbic system sends the aroma through our olfactory pathway is consistent," says Peter Matravers. "When it becomes complicated is when, how the person feels about the aroma is balanced against the pharmacological effect of the aroma. Peppermint should be uplifting. But this person has had a bad experience with peppermint—now we're dealing with the conscious and the unconscious at the same time."

Aveda's pursuit of aroma is one more way to create an icon. There are others.

"We try to find a character that is connected with the brand in some intrinsic way," says David Altshul of Character LLC, formerly of Will Vinton, the company that helped give us the California Raisins. "That people can connect with in some way. And has some real conflict. Story is about character, and usually the connection with the brand is that conflict."

Altshul cites the M & M characters as being ideal because they mirror our own human love/hate relationship with chocolate. "The great brands all have some fundamental human story underlying them that connects with some human truth central to the character," he explains. "The M & Ms have a perpetual-motion conflict that's tied to the brand: You have these characters who crave attention, knowing that when they get the attention, the audience will eat them alive. So the M & Ms always run away."

Branding is narrative. It involves a person who did something, tried something, thought something, or felt some way about something. "The reason they're tied to the brand is because it's tied to an underlying human truth—we want

things that are bad for us. M & Ms offer the perfect solution—
they're offered in bite-sized amounts."

Characters are participating in an ongoing story. "You
don't have to have a recurring iconic character," says Altshul.
"Nike has many characters, from Penny to Tiger Woods.
They are characters that continue the Nike story." Like the
iconic Nike swoosh, these stars are embedded with the values
and relevance of Nike.

There are basically two umbrella metaphors in advertising, explains Altshul: the metaphor of war and the metaphor
of science, or some combination of the two. (There is also the
metaphor of the gift.) But, he says, those metaphors are not
about the emotional connection you're trying to make. The
war metaphor is about competitive measures. What role does
the consumer play in the war metaphor? Everything is flying
overhead, above them, and they are huddled in the trenches.
What is the consumer's role in the science metaphor? They're
the lab rats. And the consumer's role in the gift metaphor?
They're indentured by a token bribe. Those metaphors are
actually blocking ones when it comes to making an emotional connection with consumers, says Altshul.

"The human brain has evolved to look for meaning in a
sequence of events; that's what meaning is," reveals Althsul.
"Our minds have evolved to understand complex events.
The search for meaning is a more powerful one than product
attributes can display. What people are asking when they ask
the brand question is, Who cares? Why does it have meaning
in my life? How does it connect with how I see myself in my
world? It may be an empty promise, but it's the juice." Classic T.V. characters like Tony the Tiger were born in an era

when you could reach 85 percent of the population. Television at that time occupied a different place in the culture; it was enough for Tony to simply be on television to have credibility. Today's audience doesn't buy that; they are more sophisticated, more skeptical.

"Characters like that seem empty, hollow, and vacuous today," agrees David Sproxton, executive chairman/cofounder of Aardman Animations in Bristol, England. Aardmann created the *Wallace & Gromit* television series and the film *Chicken Run* and has received three Oscars and seven nominations. "Real characters have real problems," says Sproxton. "That's what makes them more lovable. They're not perfect; they have to figure their lives and their relationships out. That makes them more likable, because you relate to their problems."

Sproxton goes back to comedy roots and cites Charlie Chaplin. "He's not living in a stylized world, he's not living in a fantasy world. He's doing what most of us do, trying to get a job, trying to make a living, trying to survive in an everyday fashion. What we have in the back of our mind, Can you put this character into any situation? and Do you know what his behavior will be? How will he react to it? That's what your story will be." Sproxton adds, "Look at *Cheers* or *Friends*. They are very everyday situations in many ways, and the comedy comes out of how these people cope with problems that we all have."

From Charley the tuna to Wal-Mart's smiley face, developing characters to represent brands has become a staple in marketing communications. However, there's a lot of wishful thinking when someone thinks that just by slapping an iconic character onto their product it will help differentiate them and be relevant. "People find us because they have a tactical problem," sums David Altshul. "Should they con-temporize it, should they put a baseball cap on it—should they put the baseball cap on backward? Then they under-stand that it's a much deeper set of questions. We concentrate on the thing that we can make tangible and own. It's all about focus." Real stories, well told.

Tiger Woods has become a valuable icon for Nike. Only rarely is he seen without his Nike baseball cap or other Nike gear. Tiger Woods and Nike have become inseparable, in ways that perhaps only Michael Jordan and Nike can rival. The question is whether or not this is an asset or a liability, both for the corporate sponsor and for Tiger Woods. "One of the things that's challenging for us," says Alastair Johnston of IMG, the management company that handles Tiger Woods, "is how you build Tiger Woods the brand without being dominated by any one of his licensees. Particularly Nike. So, in the process, we are building a Tiger Woods identification concurrently and in collaboration with Nike."

At best, weighing the demands of current licensing and future plans is a difficult prospect. Will Tiger Woods remain a Nike icon or will he become a restaurateur like Jack Dempsey, Michael Jordan, Mickey Mantle, and other faded sports luminaries? Will he start a winery like Mario Andretti, design golf courses like Jack Nicklaus, or create a clothing line like Arnold Palmer (Note: in a reverse cultural flip-flop, the target for the Arnold Palmer line of clothing in Japan is teenage girls). Marketers like Target and Absolut vodka and

Volkswagen have used their iconic logo and bottle and car shapes artfully, with an authority and self-confidence that would make most marketers blush. Marketing the Apple iPod has created a visual style on television and in print advertising that is remarkable eye glue and markedly iconic. Created by TBWA\Chiat\Day art director Susan Alinsangan and writer Tom Kraemer, Susan's layout of a white cord against a black silhouette was originally part of a small assignment to do a billboard campaign. Everyone thought it looked cool. "Later," says Tom Kraemer, "Lee Clow [worldwide creative director and chairman] suggested we get money from Steve Jobs to do a test to see what it would look like as a TV spot. Once we saw that we all realized it was unique. You couldn't take your eyes off it."

There are also icons that signal accomplishment. These are the trophies and ribbons and medallions awarded to winners. The Medal of Honor. The Oscar. The Nobel Prize medallion. Bronze, silver, and gold Olympics medals. The pink Cadillacs awarded to top-selling Mary Kay cosmetic salespeople. The black robes of Oxford dons. The retirement watch. The supersized check for lottery winners. The Heisman trophy, the Stanley Cup, the high school diploma, the graduate's cap and gown, the bishop's miter, the horseshoe of flowers placed around Kentucky Derby winners. These victory icons symbolize the triumphs of achievement that people struggle and make sacrifices for. The icons sometimes have their own primal code, as the histories, creed, and rituals and rites of passage endured to achieve the victory icon are revealed. They also have their own set of pagans (the clearest being failure to achieve the icon) and special words that are engaged to achieve the icon's special status. Dozens of Hollywood films have told the stories of sport athletes, movie and theater actors, race car drivers, horse jockeys, and others who have suffered and sacrificed in order to obtain the fame and recognition that comes with possession of these icons.

Icons evolve over time. The icon of a suit of armor, for example, meant war and death and destruction to those living in 1452. To the contemporary observer, the metal plates are an icon of the medieval age or, more likely, an icon of romantic chivalry, if not simply a symbol of dusty museums. Icons can use any of the five senses—sight, taste, smell, touch, sound—to become memorable and have meaning. But again, they are only a part of the primal code. Through the history of marketing many have felt that discovering the right icon alone is the path to greatness. The city of St. Louis, for example, has the arch. While other cities may envy the arch and aspire to mimic it, the arch alone does not have people flocking to visit St. Louis or aching to live there. In order to create something that people believe in and want to belong to, all elements of the primal code must be active. It is not enough to create a flag. You must have a nation willing to follow it.

The Rituals

We are all familiar with major life rituals like weddings, funerals, Fourth of July parades, graduation ceremonies, and religious rites. But our daily lives are filled with other key ritualistic behaviors. The way we drive to work in the morning, whether we brew our coffee or stop at Starbucks, how we shop for groceries, whether or not we vote and how we vote, whether we watch Letterman or Leno are all minirituals that make up the human drama of our day on the planet.

Rituals are the repeated interactions that people have with your enterprise. Doing the laundry is a highly ritualized cleansing task, driving your car can be a ritualized act of freedom, two enterprises that marketers like Unilever and General Motors have engaged anthropologists to study at length. Some rituals, like making the bed or brushing your teeth, are part of the drone of everyday life. Other rituals may not even seem ritualized, since they are acted out so few times over the course of a lifetime. Buying a mattress, shopping for insurance, installing new carpet, moving a household, going to the dentist, buying a new home are ritual events that contain important touch points that signal good and bad experiences.

Some rituals vital to their business are ignored by marketers. When we take the car to be serviced for its ten-thousand-mile checkup it's a ritual (Saturn and Chevrolet owners expect different components in that ritual, for example, than BMW and Mercedes owners). Doctor and dentist appointments are rituals. When we punch numbers on the telephone to contact our bank or airline or telephone company, those are rituals. (A recent study claims that we can punch in over one hundred numbers in order to transfer funds from one bank account to another, a frustrating ritual that could be simpler.) Logging onto the Internet is a ritual. Searching on Google is a ritual.

Ritual replaces chaos with order. Rituals are active engagements that can be imbued with either positive or negative meaning. In fact, the vitality of your brand comes with the number of positive interactions you have with your consumer. When customers walk into REI stores they are greeted with a climbing wall that says just about everything a retailer selling outdoors equipment needs to say. Cold Stone Creamery has transformed scooping ice cream into a joyful rite of blending chocolate chunks, M&Ms, peanut butter, and other ingredients over a cold marble slab. When a classical radio station put callers on hold during its annual fund drive, they were treated to a live in-studio performance of Beethoven.

Rituals are touch points with your brand and ideology that might be made more pleasant, more engaging, enhanced, simplified, less frustrating, or more fun. Consider wrestling. The only difference between the wrestling that anthropologist Claude Lévi-Strauss studied fifty years ago and contemporary wrestling is how today's events have been amped up and put on Hollywood steroids. The staged arena entry, the interviews, the masks, the ritualized holds have now been put to heavy-metal music and camera angles usually reserved for kung fu movies. The result is that World Wrestling Entertainment is watched by millions more viewers around the planet.

The workplace has rituals, too. And it's not just gathering around the water cooler or the annual company picnic. Project meetings, performance reviews, sales meetings, conventions, meeting with vendors, lenders, unions, and customers are all necessary and important rituals in the day-to-day life of a company. When large corporations merge—as they have so often in the last decade—they bring with them a collision of competing rituals. Monday morning meetings, holiday celebrations, management retreats, budgeting processes, the morning coffee stop all become fair game in the soupy mix of clashing corporate cultures. The truth is that the spirit of both companies is built, in part, around those seemingly unimportant rituals. Their sudden loss or diffusion results in confused employees, loss of focus, misdirection, and plainly dispirited groups. Productivity suffers, valuable people leave for other jobs ("It's just not the same here any more"), and the new corporate entity becomes an anomalous mass no one identifies with. Company leaders have the difficult task of deciding which rituals are important and meaningful and should seep into the new corporate host. They must also determine what new rituals might be created to replace old ones. This is a daunting but critically important task.

Rituals also note the passing of time. New Year's Eve marks the passing from one year into the next. Weddings celebrate the union of two individuals into a marriage. Funerals note the passing into another world. Smoke outside the Vatican marks the introduction of a new pope. The bloody sheet hung outside the royal bedchamber in olden times marked the king's ritual with his virgin bride and heralded a new era. And so, too, does the president's inaugural address. Tearing down the Berlin Wall was a ritual tearing down of the Soviet Republic. Its action was as symbolic as French revolutionaries tearing down markers of French aristocracy or Vandals knocking down the statuary of Roman senators. The tearing down, although maddening and even violent, is a ritual of change.

In the hubbub of modern life rituals can often be over-looked or understated. But they are no less important today than they were two thousand years ago. The entry of a new car onto the market, the introduction of a new service, a new way of thinking, or the end of apartheid are moments in time that can be accompanied by ritual acts that highlight the moment. In fact, taking the chaff of everyday life—the seem-ingly ordinary events in our daily routine—and turning them into special moments is what helps successful mar-keters stand out. How to pour a Guinness. Applauding the new Saturn car buyer. How Martha Stewart bakes a cookie. These are all ritualistic behaviors that are incorporated into the primal branding construct. The real power is under-standing how rituals can be tweaked and made more inter-esting, more evolved, or otherwise better suited to their purposes.

On its own, Billund, Denmark, seems an unlikely place to attract visitors. A few hundred miles from Copenhagen, the land is flat. Thin trees and drainage ditches outline the perimeter of emerald farm fields. In a nearby church a sailing ship hangs above the altar, a pledge for prayers for safe pas-sage. The wind does not stop in Billund. It sweeps straight through from Greenland and the chilling North Atlantic and across the Danish peninsula and the Russian flats toward Asia. But on any summer's day, when wisps of white cloud skid across blue skies, the excited cries of children can be heard as they scamper through a place called LEGOLAND.

Billund is worldwide headquarters for the Lego Corpora-tion, a company started back in 1932 by Ole Kirk Kristiansen, a man who carved wooden ducks and fire engines for children. (Lego actually stands for the Danish *"leg godt,"* which means "play well.") In 1949, Ole's son Gottfried discovered a company producing a plastic building brick in the United Kingdom. He purchased their tools and intellectual property, then invented the tubes inside the Lego block. He asked a toy store owner what was missing in the toy industry. The owner replied that no one really had a toy system. Gottfried quickly filled the gap with his plastic bricks, and his toy system spread from Denmark throughout Europe. In England and Germany Lego continues to be one of the most popular toys for boys age two to seven (only Italy is resistant to the orderly plastic blocks).

Today, people around the world snap together Lego blocks to form dinosaurs, cities, and whatever else takes hold of their imagination. More often than not it is a continuing ritual. Visit any of the hundreds of Web sites constructed by Lego enthusiasts and you can imagine people hunkered in their basements on long winter nights, snapping together fantasy worlds from bits of pronged plastic. (According to Lego headquarters, if you have six of the eight-tubed Lego blocks, you can combine them in 900 million different ways.) There are over 9 million hits for Lego on Google. From Lego chat rooms to The Brick Testament by the Reverend Brendan Powell Smith (a site "in no way sponsored, authorized or endorsed by the Lego company") to a Lego club in Chilliwack, British Columbia, enthusiasts post photos of their latest Lego creations online, and reveal their Lego mania and a brand zealotry that Ole Kirk Kristiansen probably never dreamed possible.

Toy merchants entering Lego headquarters are received in an airy expanse that is testimony to both the worlds of modern Danish design and childlike fantasy. The sparse white walls are accented with Lego sculptures of dinosaurs, attractive abstract shapes, Lego wall art, even Darth Vader, all created from Lego blocks. A beautiful modern amphitheater has been constructed for corporate presentations and new product unveilings.

For a time, one area of the building was particularly exceptional, with a doorway that led into a special fantasy world. To enter, visitors first donned unibody clean suits and slipped on paper hospital booties. Middle-aged toy buyers and retail guests suddenly found themselves dressed like new fathers about to enter the birthing room. That was exactly the point. One by one, road warriors stepped into a rebirthing process. In the first room a television blared about war and violence and the chaos of humankind. A table and chair set hanged upside down from the ceiling: The world had been turned upside down and inside out. The next room was the birthing room, and a woman giving birth screamed on an audio track. The exit door was lined with broom bristles, representing a vaginal portal. Within the next hundred steps visitors were led through the growing process, from a room that contained a forest of oversized pant legs representing the toddler stage (with an odd sense of Danish humor, one of the adults actually farted), to a fork in the road as males and females headed toward their adolescent destinies. The birthing rooms stayed up for several years, guiding middle-aged toy merchants back to the age when they might have played with Lego themselves.

Now imagine your typical visit to staid company head-quarters. Enough said. Lego is a company that is all about imagination, about re-creating the world in 900 million different ways. What better way to express that notion than to have businessmen and women deconstruct their middle-aged perspectives and return to the age that their school-aged customers experience every day?

The consequence of engineering positive rituals around your product or service while your competitors conduct business as usual can have positive effects on your business. Other examples.

Traffic is backed up on the Ventura Freeway. As drivers edge past an automobile accident they are surprised to see not only smashed vehicles, but also a van bearing a Progressive Insurance sign. As rubberneckers roll by the collision, they watch the Progressive claims adjuster write a check to his client for the damage.

Thanks to Progressive Insurance the painful ritual of calling your insurance company after an accident has been taken to a different level. Progressive decided that even the competitive (if perhaps boring) world of insurance could be infused with fresh thinking.

"Progressive came up with three concepts," says Alan Bauer, president of Progressive Direct. "A 24/7 claims service, 24/7 customer service, and rate comparison service."

Sending people to the scene to issue a check and resolve claims on the spot is a big differentiator for Progressive. There are other smart business reasons why Progressive takes the ritual of accident claims to a different level. "We actually get a lot of ancillary business with noninsureds who have been in accidents with Progressive insureds," claims a former Progressive manager (in plain English, that means they get people to switch to Progressive). "It's a part of why people know us and why we get a lot of word-of-mouth marketing buzz around our brand." And in an industry where risk assessment is everything, sending your own people to the site during the confused jumble of postaccident trauma can help reduce the scope of claims, the likelihood of misrepresentation, and other costly events.

"A lot of the company's focus is about enhancing the customer's experience and doing things that other companies just wouldn't do," says a former manager. Progressive's mission is to reduce the human trauma and economic cost of automobile accidents. And they are continually testing new products with that focus.

"Writing the check doesn't really end the story for the consumer," says Alan Bauer. "The consumer still has a wrecked car." And the consumer still has to deal with body shops, getting a rental car, and all the other hassles. So Progressive is rolling out a program where you hand over your car keys and they hand you the keys to a rental car plus a beeper. Progressive handles the body shop, inspects their work, and beeps you when your car is ready. "The amount of emotional hassle drops a lot," says Bauer. "Even if you're not a Progressive customer, we try and see if we can do this for you." Currently in twenty cities, the program is rolling out nationwide.

Progressive has innovated around the painful ritual tasks of shopping for insurance and making claims. Their innovation has paid off. In the last decade they have become the third largest automobile insurer in the United States.

Philips Medical is the world leader in medical diagnostic imaging equipment. In a recent alliance with Advocate Lutheran General Children's Hospital in greater Chicago, Philips began turning the impersonal ritual of getting a CAT scan, MRI, or X-ray into patient-friendly participation. "What we're doing with design is moving from machines to experience," says George Marmaropoulos, Philips's design director. The imaging process has traditionally been one of removing control from the patient. Stripped of street clothes, jewelry, and their dignity, patients enter the MRI experience with dread and anxiety. So Marmaropoulos and his team have used Philips technology to engineer an "ambient experience" in an attempt to give control back to the patient. "The main idea," says Marmaropoulos, "is to move from the paradigm of the patient to the paradigm of the hotel."

The analogy may be inexact, but the execution is an improvement in patient care that reduces patient anxiety, stress, and need for sedation. Using Philips lighting and consumer electronics, children can choose from preselected environments like nature, water themes, even outer space. They can also select their own music and what movie to watch. When they enter an imaging suite in the radiology ward (the walls are curved to make the room more friendly), each child waves a card over a reader. The room transforms floor to ceiling into the environment the child has selected. Rather than sterile cold walls heaped with medical equipment, this self-created light zone immediately puts the child at ease.

"Because we are projecting what they chose, the child feels they are in a welcome environment," says Marmaropoulos.

There is no hard data yet, but a process expert with the hospital has done baseline measurements in sedation rates, patient satisfaction, staff satisfaction, and clinical efficiency. Psychologists and other hospital researchers, however, look forward to a reduction in the number of patients who need to be sedated, which reduces costs and risks to patients, especially children. They also expect a reduction in the number of canceled appointments from anxious patients. Another expected advantage is a more efficient workflow for the staff, thanks to better patient cooperation.

Part of the experience is instructional. When kids squirm, CAT scans, X-rays, and MRIs become blurred, meaning the process has to be repeated, resulting in increased costs as well as increased radiation exposure and possible health risks. However, in the ambient outer space environment, for example, when the child is supposed to hold their breath, the on-screen space alien holds its breath and encourages the child to do likewise.

"It really moves the whole medical technology discipline into the human element," says Janet Ensign, program manager for North America for Philips Medical Systems. "The focus is usually on technical performance, which is what we concentrate on. This lets us look at how people use and experience the equipment and how we can take into account the human element." In other words, it's beyond product ergonomics; this time it's about soul.

Of course, what they can do in scanning rooms, Philips can stage throughout the hospital environment. Hospital corridors lack natural light, which creates a less than ideal work environment, so one Philips technology that Marmaropoulos imagines are lights that replicate the natural rhythms of daylight. Aromas in staging areas might also enhance the ambient experience. If Marmaropoulos can continue to work his magic in parking lots, waiting lounges, doctor's offices, and inpatient rooms as he intends, one day we might actually look forward to going to the doctor.

Defining the rituals involved with your product, service, personality, or function is an important step in adding meaning and relevance to your brand.

At Butterfield & Robinson, a destination experience company whose trips can run one hundred thousand dollars or more (they are quick to add that most trips are priced at four figures), the ritual of escape is an art form. After an afternoon hiking up the steep walls of the Grand Canyon during one departure (in B&R vernacular a trip is the route taken, not the journey; see "sacred words"), exhausted Butterfield & Robinson travelers were greeted with a celebratory bottle of chilled champagne. Standing on the rim overlooking the vastness of the Grand Canyon and easing their sore muscles, hikers clinked glasses and smiled. Next to them, another group of trekkers looked on, tired and thirsty.

"Who are you people?" the other group asked.

"We're Butterfield & Robinson," came the bubbly reply. Same trip, different rituals. Same trip, different experiences.

The importance of ritual can be seen not only in terms of presenting quality experiences, but in repeat performances. At Canyon Ranch, an exclusive spa where even first-time guests are greeted by name, personalized service is an art form. "It is a caring service, rather than a customer service," says Carl Pratt, managing director at Canyon Ranch in Lenox, Massachusetts. (Another ranch is in Tucson, while Las Vegas and the *Queen Mary* enjoy Canyon Ranch spa facilities.)

Guests can enjoy the same room as their last trip, and often prefer to be treated to a routine that is the same year after year. Pratt tells the story of how a new management team tried to change the daily meditation schedule from five o'clock in the afternoon to eight o'clock in the morning. Ranchers were up in arms. They'd been doing their same routine for years, longtime guests argued, and they refused to change. The meditation hour was moved back to its original five o'clock slot, and management found other ways to enhance the guest experience.

Weiden+Kennedy, the advertising agency that has helped shape Nike's culture over the last twenty years, also has its own corporate culture. When the agency was still young, newcomers were cheerfully introduced to the rest of the staff in a ritual welcoming at the local watering hole. At the end of the event the surprised newcomer was told that he or she was stuck paying for the bar tab. "The more we grew, the bigger the crowd," smiles one longtime staffer. "There were some pretty big tabs." And the work rituals didn't stop there. "During lunch, people would go off and play basketball or work out in the company gym," says Catherine McIntyre-Velky, former head of W+K's traffic department. "Then we'd go back to work, still sweating, and didn't change clothes. It was pretty hard-core."

These team-building experiences created an Us versus

Them mentality. Just because you were *on* the team didn't mean you were a *part* of the team. In the highly competitive advertising arena, these workplace rituals resolved that question.

The traditional sales call is a necessary task that drives the fortunes of major companies around the world and is often overlooked as a ritual. But at Z-Brand, a breakthrough line of high-fashion clothing where the T-shirts can go for eighty to a hundred dollars, the sales call ritual receives a provocative new twist. Instead of hiring traditional salespeople, Z-Brand hired people under thirty who live the image of what their clothing is trying to portray. Called "nomads," these young people are willing to throw a pair of jeans into a mosh pit at night and meet a Nordstrom's buyer by day. "We weren't looking for kids that had experience in selling or marketing, we were looking for kids who were passionate about a particular lifestyle," says Z-Brand marketing director Bryan Johnson. "We wanted them to a) wear the product and b) go out and find the retail accounts we were going after."

Armed with a cell phone, a laptop computer, and a digital camera, nomads scoured the East and West Coasts and delivered Z-Brand's first impression at store level. Out of Z-Brand's over 500 accounts, 450 of them have been engaged through nomads. "Their mission is to go to events," says Johnson. "Whether it's a frat party, a hip club, a bar, a fashion show, a county fair, rock concert, both indoor arenas and outdoor, any event they know that's going on. To be a part of that event and place our product on the hip, cool people at whatever event they're at. Not to just give away product to anybody who's got their hands out, but specifically seek out the trendsetter or the leader of the group and to place product on them. In addition to that, get product placed on the bands, actors, or actresses, anybody that is a key image person that would be good for the brand. And that has been going phenomenally well."

So who's been spotted wearing Z-Brand? "Sean Penn, Britney Spears, Madonna, Seal, Bruce Willis, Van Halen, it goes on and on," says Johnson. "Through their work, nomads have placed product on people that surround these people and it's become visible to where a lot of those high-end actors and actresses or musicians have sought our product out through the hipper retailers who we have sold because of it."

Z-Brand is in numero uno retailers like the Atrium in New York City, Fred Siegal's in Hollywood, and Theodor in Beverly Hills. "We hit our goal of trying to be in four hundred doors within the first year," says Johnson.

When daughter Kelly and I decided to fly to London and visit family friends, we flew Virgin Air. Expecting a low-cost mass shuttle, we were surprised when they handed us a plastic shoulder sack filled with goodies, which Kelly explored with glee. Sitting in coach, we were surprised to find television screens on the back of every seat. Even the small knob that holds the meal tray in place was not made of industrial-grade gray plastic, but was Lego-like red. In flight, they served Virgin Cola (naturally) as we listened to tunes and watched in-flight movies. Virgin had decoded the flight experience and made the ritual of flight more interesting and more enjoyable.

The ritual of flight will become even more dramatic if Richard Branson can boost his Virgin Galactic off the ground. The mission of this spaceline is to offer the world's first commercial space flights, which will become available to ordinary people within the next five years, according to Branson. Space tourists will travel at supersonic speed to greet the sublime darkness of interstellar space.

When guests walk into any one of the over seven thousand Aveda salons around the world they are not just greeted with a tray of herbal teas. When customers move to the back of the store they are welcomed with what marketing VP Chris Hacker calls a "hand treatment," which he quickly explains is a scalp massage.

"The scalp massage is a critical part of what we do," says Hacker. "Because we want the person to relax, to feel comfortable, to be open and stimulated in such a way that allows them to communicate really well with the stylist. When touch happens, we build a more instant connection."

Recently, Davin Stowell at Smart Design started working with HP on a series of products. In the sexier-than-thou world of computer products Stowell stepped back and took a deep breath. Today, most computers, as well as printers, scanners, and other accessories, are shipped directly to the end user. Without an on-site installer to make sure the products function properly the product must be ready to go right out of the box, with as little box-to-operational time as possible.

"What will really make a difference to you," says Stowell (speaking specifically about HP printers), "is what the experience is from the moment you take the product out of the box until you get your first print. Our goal is to have that [have somebody pull it out of the box and be able to start printing pictures without reading the instructions] happen in less than a minute." Products that can achieve that, says Stowell, can be more effective than whatever eye-catching design skin the product might have, or what sexy-looking box it inhabits.

"I think back on my various cell phones," he laughs, "and I'm on my third one since the one that was really easy to use. The ones that I have now may look cooler, but what I remember is the one that was easiest to use."

Rituals are the meaningful repeated points of contact between you and your guest, customer, client, or target market. The weekly trip to the grocery store. Back-to-school shopping. Christmas shopping. Shopping for Valentine's Day or buying groceries for the Thanksgiving feast are rituals in themselves. These interactions with the customer can be flat experiences, or they can serve as enriching touch points that excite consumers and intensify the brand experience.

Sainsbury's in London has a special drop-off zone for toddlers so Moms can shop unimpeded. Wal-Mart and Best Buy shoppers are met by greeters as they enter the store. Rituals are the repeated interactions that you have with your customers. These interactions may be positive, or they may be negative. Consider the hundreds of keystrokes necessary to balance your checkbook, resolve a credit card problem, or simply reach a human being by phone at many corporations. Some things you don't even think of as ritual. Events like using an ATM machine, buying something on the Web, calling your doctor, booking a flight, going to the dry cleaners, going to the Laundromat are all rituals that can either smack of pleasure or pain.

Red Wing Shoe Company, a one-hundred-year-old manufacturer based in Red Wing, Minnesota, takes the seemingly simple act of buying work boots to its own level of ritual. The first rite is to make sure customers have the right product. "Half the product that fails to perform is because they have a boot or shoe that's not made for the task," explains David Murphy, president and chief operating officer at Red Wing. "That's a big deal. If you're a logger, you need boots that have a high heel and a rugged sole. Ironworkers need perfect balance; they use a wedge sole that's very soft, so if their foot is slightly off the beam, they can feel it. If you work on a chicken farm," says Murphy, "chicken shit is incredibly acidic; you need the proper materials. So the first thing we do is ask, What do you want it for?"

The second part of the ritual is fitting. "Most people are buying general shoes so they don't need a precise fit," says Murphy. "The materials are soft, so your foot mashes it down anyway. That's not true for Red Wing. When you welt down a sole it doesn't give. You put a steel toe in a boot, it doesn't break in. If you design a boot with a certain heel lift, or a pull-on boot, the shape of the heel is critical. We build our boots so precisely, the fit is critical, very different than it is for different kinds of shoes. This is the kind of boot I need to do my job."

The proper way to measure, Murphy explains, is with a Brannock Foot Measuring Device, which is in all five hundred Red Wing shoe stores. "Feet are like snowflakes," contends

Murphy. "You can take ten people that all measure size 9 in length and scan their foot profile and they're all different. You haven't accounted for their instep, the width of their foot, the length of their toes." Red Wing manufactures twenty-seven thousand SKUs that include five hundred styles of boots from size 5A to 20EEEE. The company spends over half a million dollars a year training their specialists so they know what boot or shoe to put customers in. And it's because of the fitting ritual that Red Wing does not sell shoes and boots online.

"It's not just a ritual that exists because it's neat or fun or part of our heritage. It has real value. It's not the ribbon on the package," says Murphy. "It *is* the package."

The Pagans, or Nonbelievers

In order to have the yin of believers you must also have the yang of nonbelievers. The pagans. The heathens and idolaters. Part of saying who you are and what you stand for is also declaring who you are not and what you don't stand for. The contrasting counterparts of Democrats are Republicans. There are hawks and doves. Pro-life and pro-choice. DOS/Java. National Rifle Association/the Brady Campaign. Internet/bricks and mortar. Cola/un-cola. Organic/processed. Gas guzzlers/tree huggers. New York/L.A. The sacred and the profane.

We live in a world that has defined itself by contrast and paradox for thousands of years. Trend master Robyn Waters tells about a trip to Angor Wat, where she encountered a temple doorway adorned with eighty-eight gods and ninety-eight demons portrayed in a desperate tug-of-war. The churning they created in the struggle is the froth of life, a battle between opposites carved into stone a thousand years ago.

Defining your pagans is important in defining who you are. This can be difficult when marketers do not want to exclude potential customers and mass markets. After all, who doesn't believe in health care, potato chips, or bottled water? Well, probably people who want faster, more personable medical treatment, organic foodies, and soda pop drinkers. Finding your antithesis and proceeding to vilify them is a common positioning tool, whether they are your competing product, ideology, or political opponent. The first thing Premier Nikita Khrushchev did when he followed Stalin to power was denounce Stalin as a criminal. Thirty years ago, 7Up declared itself the "uncola." Today, Taco Bell encourages people to "think outside the bun." Apple Computer twisted IBM's famous "Think" mandate by encouraging people to "think different."

Once you understand who the pagans are—those who do not and perhaps never will understand you—you open up new opportunities to be who you are and manifest your potential for what you can become. People who drink Starbucks in the morning probably aren't going to care for Folgers Instant. Yankees fans are not Red Sox fans. (And vice versa.) People who find their leisure in exclusive mountain lodges usually do not tug trailer homes. The pagans for the hundreds of public libraries in the country are people who use the Internet and, more specifically, Google. A decade or more ago people either bought American-made or foreign-made automobiles. With today's mass globalization and automobile assembling technologies that friend/pagan dichotomy has become less valid, as most cars today are a combination of ignition systems, transmissions, and body parts coming from all parts of the globe. Nevertheless, if there's a Ford parked in your garage, there's probably not a Chevrolet sitting next to it. If you're on a heart-healthy diet, products high in fat and cholesterol are anathema.

Most often, the people who do not believe are easily identifiable. By being what you are not they help crystallize what you believe and what you can become. Like Romans and Christians, Allies and Axis, Yankees and Red Sox we vilify and deny their beliefs. We expurgate those who belong to the pagan cause and rejoice and celebrate our own beliefs as we surround ourselves with those who belong to our cause.

The Sacred Words

All belief systems come with a set of specialized words that must be learned before people can belong. If you're a marathon runner you understand what it means to "hit the wall." If you are a computer user you understand what it means to "log on," what a "virus" is, and what it means to "crash." If you go to Starbucks you understand the difference between a "tall" and a "grande." To follow the world of Walt Disney you learned the songs and memorized names like Minnie Mouse, Goofy, Pluto, and Donald Duck. Perhaps you even taught yourself to speak like Donald. To obtain your membership in American culture you memorized lines from the Declaration of Independence, the Gettysburg Address, and *Seinfeld.* You memorized phrases from the Bible, the Talmud, the Quran to become a member of your faith. You learned the baseball stats that are the lexicon of faith for leagues of baseball enthusiasts.

Words tell who we are. Doctors, lawyers, advertising professionals, actors, carpenters, computer analysts, butchers, pharmacists, and car mechanics all have professional terminology, some might say jargon, and have sacred words that must be known to belong within that group. One film director described the learning process that helped him transit from a successful still photographer to becoming a successful moving picture director: "Know the words." Therefore, sacred words are not simply professional jargon but crucial to understanding a technical process. While they are technical terms of art, those same words also bind people together as a group and are often crucial to working together effectively.

Many products and services have words dedicated to their use or process. If you intend to order a Big Mac instead of a Whopper you know where you need to be. iPod, iMac, and iLife have become sacred code for Apple enthusiasts. If you are a member of the professional industrialized world and someone asks you to FedEx something, you know what needs to be done.

Author Mark Abley talks about the use of language to help create culture in his book *Spoken Here: Travel Among Threatened Languages.* Traveling among remote peoples around the planet Abley witnessed the gradual and sometimes sudden erosion of a tribe's sense of identity when the native language is taken away. An example: Off the coast of Wales is a small island called the Isle of Man. For thousands of years the island was home to the Manx language and culture, largely intact until the nineteenth century. With the burst of tourists and other outsiders in the 1900s the natives could not survive the encroachment. Finally, in 1974, the last Manx speaker died.

However. "There is a very determined group of people spanning the generations who have succeeded to some extent in reviving the Manx language," says Abley. "These people have fastened on language specifically as a means of reviving the Manx culture."

Says Abley, "I remember one man said to me, 'Everything that we can think of specifically Manx, that is, specifically belonged to the island, whether it be the music, or the folk-lore, other cultural traditions, it all hangs on the language.'"

Traveling around the planet the inquisitive traveler will find remote peoples whose language serves to define them. The Manx, the Damin, the Mohawk, and the South Bronx are not much different from the languages of people who inhabit the secular worlds of Nike, Apple, IBM, Starbucks, and Hollister. While traditional linguists might recoil at the thought the fact is that language helps to define and distinguish us from others.

"The thing about language," says Abley, "is that there's always going to be a need for groups to identify themselves and set themselves apart somehow. We live in a society which is incredibly complex and the only way to deal with that is to feel a part of a subgroup or to make ourselves an extended family generally, and so one of the really good ways to do that is to baffle outsiders."

ttyl g2g 2wk lyl.

Any teenager in American can tell you that the above cryptogram says, "Talk to you later, gotta go to work, love you lots." These are the sacred words of the subscribers to AOL's Instant Messenger service, a virtual community that millions of teenagers log onto every day. Sitting at the keyboard after school, at night, on weekends, IM kids have invented their own language, totally in keeping with the rapid-fire nanochatter compliant with IM, where kids keep several conversations going at once. The best way to do that—at least the solution they have invented for themselves—is to create their own abbreviated language that lets them type out replies in speedy nanobits.

If you know the language, you belong. Perhaps the most isolating aspect of getting old is not just the aging process, but the fact that as language evolves, the word set for your worldview is slowly and inexorably replaced. So slowly, in fact, that you are hardly aware. Before you know it you're still talking horse-and-buggies while the rest of the world is living in cyberspace. Suddenly, no one wants to talk to Grandma. Not because they don't love Grandma, but because grandmother and grandchild no longer share a common tongue.

brb

Trend watchers invariably form their own patois. The amalgamate verbage of "massclusivity," "nouveau niche," "pop-up

retail," "mass class," "snobmoddities," and "planned spontane-
ity" form a utilitarian thinkspeak as they define the jumble of
colliding events in the popstream.

"Bling" is a sacred word.

Many sacred words are invented constructions. iPod. Iced
grande skinny decaf latte. Bar calls like Bud, Cosmo, and Sex
on the Beach are also sacred words. So are fins, turbo, and
cam. And sauté, fold, and carmelize.

Here's a behind-the-scenes look at how one set of sacred
words was created. "I was kind of goofing around with this
Dr. Seuss thing," says Craig Tanimoto. "And I started talking
about the star-bellied sneetches and drawing all this stuff, basically just doodling, and I looked down at my pad and one of
the things I had written down was 'Think different.'" Tanimoto was an art director at advertising agency Chiat\Day's
Venice, California, office when he was called in for a secret
pitch. You have to remember back to a time before the iMac,
before the iPod, when Apple was on life support.

"They were going to bring Steve Jobs back," Tanimoto
recalls, "and they needed a campaign to get them through the
next six months. There was nothing to introduce and nothing to talk about." So Tanimoto decided there wasn't much
to do but celebrate the Mac user and make them feel more
important. "On the other side of the paper I had drawn a picture of Thomas Edison with a lightbulb above his head, so I
put the two together, like a Keith Haring pop-art illustra-
tion. The second one we did was Einstein, and then Gandhi.
Those were the first three." None of the dozen or more peo-

ple seen in the "Think different" campaign actually used an Apple computer. Instead, the campaign focused on a higher ideal, one of personal integrity, not following the common road, the message of, Hey, it's okay to be different. The campaign ran on outdoor boards, on the sides of buildings in Los Angeles and Manhattan, and in magazines. Within six months Apple introduced the iMac, company stock went through the roof, and they never looked back.

Richard Saul Wurman, who founded the TED Conferences, started each conference by saying, "Welcome to the dinner party I always wanted to have and couldn't."

The TED Conferences brought together masters from the worlds of technology, entertainment, and design during three days of intellectual hedonism that engendered its own community. "When I started TED the people there started calling themselves 'TEDsters,'" says Wurman. "I didn't make up that term, it was a self-generated word." Anyone who was new to the TED conference was called a "TED virgin." When there was a particularly resonant or enlightening moment, it was called a "TED moment." "What is interesting," says Wurman, "is that there was enough value in the word 'TED' that people developed their own language from it."

Belief systems come with their own invented lexicon that has precious meaning for those who believe. The language defines those who belong, and those who do not. Sometimes those words are secret; sometimes the sacred words are so laden with meaning that people are willing to fight and die for them.

The Leader

All successful belief systems have a person who is the catalyst, the risk taker, the visionary, the iconoclast who set out against all odds (and often against the world at large) to re-create the world according to their own sense of self, community, and opportunity. The list of such people is as long as history itself. Recent examples include people like Thomas Jefferson, Ted Turner, Richard Branson, Mohandas Gandhi, Steve Jobs, Bill Gates, Phil Knight, Dr. Martin Luther King, Nelson Mandela, Oprah, Gloria Steinem, Cesar Chavez, and others who have led companies, brands, movements, causes, and ideologies to create core groups of believers that changed the world.

The leader can be the founder, like Richard Branson, Thomas Edison, Walt Disney, or Tom Watson. Or it can be the strong individual who takes their place either functionally or symbolically. People like Jack Welch, Michael Eisner, Sam Palmisano, the pope, and every president since George Washington. Other leaders can be found within the strata of the organization: brand stewards, product managers, team leaders, production line experts, union leaders, human resources trainers, or the general manager are all important to the success or failure of the brand, company, and cause.

Enterprise without a leader is like a headless elephant. It may eventually get somewhere, but only by destroying everything in its path along the way.

So much has been written about the risks, responsibilities, and rewards of leadership there is no need to repeat tales of leadership, the heroic struggles against daunting competitors, prerevolutionary mind-sets, stoic ideologies, and other forms of evil. Yet, it should be noted that the leader's quest in the primal narrative frequently becomes mythic simply because that is the most powerful form of storytelling. No one is interested in battles against ordinary odds.

Most of the leaders we hear about have natural sizzle. People like Richard Branson, Oprah, Martha Stewart, and others are charismatic men and women who want to propel their ideas forward. However, many of today's leaders of large organizations are pulled from the ranks of finance and information technology. With rare exceptions, their personality types seem constitutionally unable to reboot their management styles on behalf of the larger mission. When these leaders turn turtle and stick to their proficiencies their bland management style inevitably shortchanges the organization long term. Companies that become favored brands are worth a multiple many times that of the bottom-line-driven organization. Statistics vary on exactly what that multiple might be, but a recent *Fast Company* article states, "Research suggests that brands that engage consumers emotionally can command prices as much as 20% to 200% higher than competitor's and sell in far higher volumes."

It's not just about vision. It's also about determination. Says Rand Miller, CEO of Cyan Worlds, creator of blockbuster computer games Myst, Riven, and Uru, "You know, honestly, the sheer will to just keep going. We have a lot of people here that are good and work hard, and I think there's a certain obligation—or there should be an obligation if somebody's running a company—to not drop and leave. One of the reasons we're here is to provide employment for people so they can have families and provide experiences and enjoy a living and survive. And regardless how creative you are, or what you're doing, that's the end result. People want to survive. It's too easy to just bail, close the doors, take my money, and run. There's something in me that's obligated to try as long as you can to keep things going. I don't know what that is, and it sounds right to me, it feels right, it's worthwhile. It's why we continue on."

"You can be a great designer," says Freeman Thomas, an acknowledged leader in car design. "But to be a leader in design you have to be a great communicator. There's a saying, An idea too soon is too late. You can scare everybody off, even though you have the vision for it. Communication is really important. How you filter ideas to your bosses and to the public. Some great design movements have happened, but they haven't been picked up by the public. You have to differentiate between being at a designer show and something that appeals to people. Not to get high and mighty is also important," says Thomas. "I find that just by being normal and hanging out and listening and being vulnerable. By putting myself into very normal situations I feel I have the better advantage of finding out what's next. You'll see people whose position is everything to them and they put this shield around them. You learn more by listening than by talking."

"Leadership is rare," says George Butterfield, founder of high-end travel experience company Butterfield & Robinson. "We have to work very hard to find people that have those qualities of making people feel comfortable, of knowing the region, of having lots and lots of fun in their soul because, after all, people are on their holidays. People often parade in with language skills and technical skills and they're not one bit interesting to us because they don't have our sense of fun, our sense of joy. We look at about four hundred to five hundred applicants a year," says Butterfield. "We hire maybe fifty. Ninety-nine percent of the leaders usually work out. Occasionally, we miss and someone doesn't get what we're doing. The whole essence of our trips depends on those leaders."

"It's great to be a wonderful communicator and it's great to be a motivator," says Gary Hirshberg, chief executive officer at Stonyfield Farms, the nation's leading organic foods company. "But given the choice between having someone be a great communicator or a great manager and having a vision, I will go with the latter every time. Leadership skills can be taught or learned or apprenticed. Having vision cannot be taught. Vision is the most powerful ingredient to being successful, and that doesn't just mean keeping people revved up, it means keeping people, period. The equity in our companies is our people."

At the end of the day (whether the end of your day is at 4:40 P.M. or 2:00 A.M.), work and career is about fulfillment and feeling good about what you do with your life. "The average superb product manager, chief financial officer, or comptroller here in the U.S. has endless options as to where they can take their skills," says Hirshberg. "But what I find when you ask people what's important to them and *really* ask it, what most folks are looking for is meaningful work. Having meaning, being able to go home and look at your kids and say, 'I'm doing something to help' goes a long way."

At creative advertising agency Mother, which has offices in London and New York City, leaders take on an unusual role. The agency took a unique look at the traditional advertising agency structure and decided it needed a redesign.

"Instead of assembling a bunch of people around the client, we've assembled problem solvers around the problem," says Mark Waite, one of four founding partners of Mother. "We have print or T.V. producers who are called 'mothers.'" The mother is the catalyst for getting assignments done on time and on budget. "Then we have the creative team who are actually writing the ads, and a strategist," says Waite. "We bring the client into that team as well."

At Mother, whose clients include Coca-Cola, Orange cellular, Miller Brewing, and the Boots pharmacy chain, there are no traditional account directors or client managers. The client speaks directly to the people doing the work. "What we've noticed," says Waite, "is even though the mother is holding the process together, clients gravitate to the person they want to deal with. We tend to let water find its own level."

The elimination of the account director position as the leader within the advertising agency hierarchy is a fundamental change in the way that an advertising agency works. "Account people didn't have a product," asserts Waite. Traditional account managers assumed leadership because they managed the budgets and led the disciplines of media, creative, and production, and often voiced the clients' concerns inside the agency. It was a job that, according to Waite, assumed little more than a talent for conversational skills. On the other hand, "Everyone in Mother has a product," says Waite. "The strategists create strategies, creative people are doing T.V. spots, print ads, and other ideas, producers are producing print ads and television commercials."

Many of Mother's clients have other agencies that still work in the traditional way. For them, Mother provides a contrast. "So many of our clients like the fact that they get to sit down with creatives. They like the fact that they get to sit down with the print producer and the T.V. producer. They feel informed, they feel involved. And it works better for us, too," Waite says about being able to lead hands-on. "The more we know about a client, the better agency we can be."

Jim Burke is a Hollywood deal-maker. He has put together deals for *King of the Hill, Ally McBeal, The Practice,* and *Dharma and Greg* plus kid raves *Full House* and *Saved by the Bell.* As executive vice president at Rysher Entertainment, he spearheaded thirty films in five years, including *Kingpin, Howard Stern's Private Parts, The Saint,* and *It Takes Two.* He coproduced the Academy Award–nominated film *Election,* and most recently has pooled his production talents with Jim Taylor and Alexander Payne, the creative forces behind the Academy Award–winning movie *Sideways.* Burke's daily challenge is to pull together people of diverse crafts and talents, then focus them toward the singular mission of creating product that people want to sit and watch. Keeping stars and crews happy on the production set amid the high-octane mix of talent, egos, and big money is a high-wire act.

"What makes it different from most other jobs, I think, is that I have to use both sides of my brain to their fullest capacity," says Burke. "You don't like to generalize, but artists tend to attract a certain personality, lawyers another personality type. The people who work on the crew are different still." His ability to shift from talking to the people financing the film to a meaningful discussion with the screenwriter requires a special skill set. "My specialty is that I have a lot of specialties," says Burke. "Most people I'm dealing with are specialists. They're a writer, filmmaker, a distribution executive, gaffers, marketing people, lawyers, finance guys. They know exactly what they do, and they see the world from their point of view. I have to be adaptable and confident enough to be able to lead in these various areas."

There is also the daily fireman aspect of production. The unexpected weather delays, production overages, the infamous star/director conflicts. "There's always a fire," says Burke. "I do the best that I can to approach it proactively, but you can only be so successful doing that. There are situations that are unknowable and you have to deal with those on the fly." Over time, Burke has realized that his polydextrous skill is what makes him valuable. "I have skills in many areas; as I grow older I realize that makes me unusual," he says. "It's what I'm good at."

Burke reflects on what is lacking in leadership today. "Courage and honesty," he says. "People are not willing to tell people what it is they really think. It happens in politics, it happens in business, and it happens all the way down the line, with rare exceptions. The problem that most people have with leaders is that they're never sure that they're getting the straight story. When you know the person at the top is not spinning, that is real leadership."

2. Primal Belonging

The products and services that people feel something toward—and buy—have a pattern or construct in place that is not always apparent but is vital brand infrastructure.

At the end of the day we all want to feel that we are a part of something larger than ourselves. As Sue Ellen Cooper, founder of the Red Hat Society, says, "It's much more fun to be part of something big." All belief systems have people who believe, advocates who feel that the brand offers a place where they can belong. That sense of belonging manifests itself in several ways. First, consumers invest themselves in your brand by purchasing products or services because they believe in them. Second, they are willing to help convince others to belong (as we know, this word of mouth is one of the oldest and best forms of advertising). Finally, advocates believe so strongly in the brand that they fiercely defend it against rivals. Try to tell a Mac user that they have to trade it for a PC. Tell a Ford truck owner that he has to drive a Chevy. And we all remember what happened when Coke tried to change their formula.

Advocates can be your customers, but they can also be coworkers, vendors, investors, subcontractors, distributors, financial organizations, and others who feel they belong to your brand.

As human beings, we are hard-wired to believe. The final objective in engineering the pattern of the creation story, creed, icons, rituals, pagans, sacred words, leader primal branding construct is to create a belief system that attracts a community. That community can surround a product or service, a personality, a social or political cause, an internal organization (read "corporate culture"), even a civic community. Properly managed, the primal construct can help you create a belief system that results in a group of evangelists committed to advocating for you through thick and thin.

Often, the most overlooked group is the people inside your own organization. If you can't get your employees to believe, how can they possibly convince others—your customers and consumers—to believe? "The latest thing that we now recognize as fundamental is internal branding, or brand engagement," says Susan Nelson at Landor. "While it's really nice to do new logos and new signs, unless you retrain employees as to what the ideas are about and the beliefs that you want your customers to have, you can't really bring it to life. Some of the more powerful programs, like the British Petroleums, do as much work internally in communicating the brand as they do externally. That's relatively new in this business. It took a while to recognize that employee behavior needs to reflect the brand as much as all your environments and expressions do."

And yet there are tremendous numbers of people who belong to brands like the United States of America, the women's movement, VW automobiles, and Costco. There are even people who advocate a certain brand of kitchen utensils. "There's a tremendous community that's built around OXO products," says David Stowell. "OXO has never done any advertising and, initially, sales were built by word of mouth. It was amazing how a six-dollar peeler was the perfect gift for people to try this, and they'd get excited about them. And the next thing you know, they're buying half a dozen of them for their friends." This grassroots reverie is the stuff of legends. "They talk about it amongst themselves," says Stowell, "and get excited about the next new product, and we're constantly getting bags full of letters from people writing in ideas and stories about how great it was for them."

"I describe myself as a bridge builder between the outside and the inside of the company," says Jake McKee, community development manager for Lego. McKee is part of a new group at Lego that works with fans to develop relationships. Started just a few years ago, Lego Direct is striving to develop people who are outside the official kid target markets, but remain active Lego enthusiasts. In other words, these are adults who spend hours clicking Lego bricks together into castles, seascapes, action figures, furniture, and whatever else their imaginations can conjure.

For years, people had been sending photographs of incredible Lego brick creations—cityscapes, dinosaurs, knights—whatever, to Lego headquarters. Their activities were treated with a quizzical raised eyebrow by Lego management. How odd that adults were playing with toys. The company remained silent.

"When I first came to the company, people would say, 'We don't really focus on the shadow market,'" says McKee. With the Internet, Lego enthusiasts began connecting on their own. (Enter the words "lego club" on Google and you'll find over eleven thousand hits.) Lego could no longer ignore its enthusiasts, and Lego Direct was born. "It's only been over the last three or four years that we have started a more ongoing interaction with the different fans," agrees Tormod Askildsen, senior director, Lego community development. "And the reason is simply because of the Web. We hadn't been aware of the fan activities taking place." Fan postings on the Internet, however, made it very clear that a lot was happening out in the world of Lego that corporate management should acknowledge.

"We've come a long way in a very short time," says McKee. "More and more often now the internal reaction is, 'That sounds good.' They understand that if we can encourage people to carry the brand further, those are good things for us." The official Lego Club has 2.3 million kids signed up. That number is augmented today by between thirty thousand to fifty thousand enthusiasts. There are also members in Europe numbering in the thousands who put together their own events.

"That's our very safe estimate," says McKee, who has been a Lego enthusiast since the age of three. Because these clubs are so grassroots, any single group could contain anywhere from five to a couple of dozen members. There is a BrickFest held in the United States every year put together by Lego enthusiasts with little, if any, involvement from Lego corporate. And there are hundreds of local events that may involve someone putting up their Darth Vader figure at the local shopping mall. "What we do for them is what they need us to do," says McKee. "We're not trying to marketing *to* them," he advises. "We market *with*." Typical involvement might be donating Lego bricks (a life-sized Darth Vader figure can include ten thousand Lego bricks). But there is also a consumer group Web site and a catalog, with more being planned.

"We've gotten to a really good place," says McKee. "The new mindset at Lego is that there are other markets out there." "And it's not just kids. So let's think about what we can do with those other markets."

The weary traveler has been biking in the French hillsides all day. He arrives in his *chambre,* exhausted, only to find that the bed has been removed. The chairs and bedside tables have also disappeared. The hotel is clearly not prepared for his arrival. He sighs. Nothing to do but chuck on fresh clothes and bring it up with management downstairs before the wine tasting. Finally, he tells the guide about his misfortune. The guide shrugs and says a few words to the staff. The staff shrugs. A truck pulls up. In the back of the truck, with linens tucked tight and end tables in place, is his fully made-up bed. The traveler grins.

He'd forgotten that he had told the guide he wanted to do something unusual to propose to his girlfriend. There are hundreds of stories like this one from the lore of Butterfield & Robinson, the high-end expedition house based in Toronto.

B&R officially started in 1966 when George Butterfield and his wife, Martha, an art historian, teamed up with Sidney Robinson (George's high school roommate and Martha's older brother) to lead a ramshackle group of forty-three students from Naples to London. They biked, hiked, and drank their way across Europe, learning much about Europe and themselves.

This began a new-style travel company. "If we didn't invent the concept," says founder George Butterfield, "we were certainly the first to make people aware that there was no disgrace in going to the great chateaus of Europe in a biking outfit rather than a Mercedes or Jaguar." Going from one great chateau to another by foot or by bike was everything a trip to Europe was supposed to be: fun, a learning experience, and relaxing. Today Butterfield & Robinson travels to over two dozen countries, and has ninety trips and up to four hundred departures. There are also Bespoke trips, which can run over a hundred thousand dollars. What's important to Butterfield & Robinson is not the number of trips they make, but the quality of the experience. They are committed to being the best, not the biggest.

"They have B&R moments," says Scott Darnell, a Wells Fargo executive who has gone on a dozen Butterfield & Robinson journeys. Those moments include elephant rides in India, watching the sunrise fish catch in Vietnam, enjoying a private dinner party in a czarist palace serenaded by a choir and orchestra. "They give me the travel experience I'm really looking for," says Darnell.

"We regard our trips as being theater," says Benson Cowan, managing director of Butterfield & Robinson. "Not travel." Many of the trips are biking or walking excursions. The pace is deliberately slow and casual, styled as groups of like-minded travelers. "We build a space in a region," reinforces Cowan. "We build a story in a region."

People who believe develop real connections, and Butterfield & Robinson travelers are no exception. They have a profound attachment to their experiences with the company. "They feel like they're shareholders," says Managing Director Cowan. "There's a very fundamental connection and sense of identity. They identify themselves on the basis of how many times they've traveled with us."

Trips abroad can be truly special in that they are not just recreational but re-creational. During the rite of passage we return home transformed, often in remarkable ways. "They're making a choice to come with us because the people who are going to be traveling with them are like-minded enough that they're going to make real connections. And they do make real connections." Says Cowan, "People meet on our trips and they become fast friends, they get married."

Sometimes the belongers are your guests, your clients, your customers. And sometimes they are the people inside your organization. If your people are not committed to your ideals, they are not going to convince others to believe.

At luxury spa Canyon Ranch new employees are taken through a five-part Platinum Guest Service Series. The orientation tells incoming staff members not only how to meet and greet clients, but enriches them with Canyon Ranch philosophy. Rule number one? Do unto others as they would like it done.

Managing over eight hundred employees and helping them keep guests pampered is not an easy task. "Some people are here for fluff and buff," says Carl Pratt. "Others are here to recover from chemotherapy." In the seclusion of Canyon Ranch guests are treated to daily exercise, healthy food, beautiful walks, even wellness lectures, all in an environment sated with calm and goodness. To help create that experience Canyon Ranch starts by hiring people who have a genuine interest in how the guests feel. For exclusive clientele accustomed to experiencing life from the front-row seats, their needs can be demanding. And they know the difference between genuine attention and pretension.

"People often tell us," says Carl Pratt, " 'Your staff really does care, as opposed to it being rehearsed.'" In many luxury categories—from food to clothing to diamonds—the sales staff cannot afford to shop at the same place where they work. Canyon Ranch mitigates this by demanding that the staff use Ranch facilities. Says Pratt, "If the staff takes advantage of a fitness activity or a lecture or a hike they receive points, which get them everything from a free massage to a paid day off."

Letting the over eight hundred employees enjoy the pampered experience side-by-side the guests is a rewarding and educational experience that builds staff awareness and morale. "It creates a community-based experience for our guests as well as our staff," says Pratt. "We do a great deal to stimulate that effort." Canyon Ranch management is also mandated to have ten points of contact with guests and ten points of contact with staff each and every day to help build relationships and rapport.

Building a sense of community is what *belonging* is all about.

In a world filled with conflict, confusion, and paradox "I

belong" is a powerful statement. The seven pieces of primal code add up to belonging, and belonging technologies can be invented by customers, too. Remember the TED Conferences, where old-time TED members referred to new members as "TED virgins." Lego enthusiasts build their own Web sites as well as their own Lego constructions. Skateboarders build their own skate parks. Some communities hold hands. Others have a beer together.

The Internet is a significant community with a membership numbering in the millions, probably including you. "People form relationships online around mutual interests," says Howard Rheingold, author of *The Virtual Community* and *Smart Mobs* (he also teaches at Stanford University). "That's the unique capability of the Internet. It connects people who don't know each other from different parts of the world. It might be a hobby or it might be deadly serious."

Wired communities forming in chat rooms and blogs— like the Lego enthusiasts mentioned earlier—is just a beginning. Ten years ago, the phenomenon of people interacting over an "internet" was a rarified event. Today it is ubiquitous. Tomorrow, it may be, well, who can say? When Pope John Paul II died in 2005 Poles decided to convene on the field where the Polish pontiff once held a mass. The gathering was created by ten people text messaging their friends to come to the field armed with a candle. Then those people text messaged ten more people. Within a few hours, one hundred thousand people met in prayer on the open field.

The convergence between cell phones, video, and data is just beginning. "I don't think the ability of people to form online groups has stopped evolving yet," says Rheingold.

Ultimately, says Rheingold, the untethered Internet in people's pockets on inexpensive devices is going to have more impact than desktop computers. "I think we'll see *another* wave of this becoming even more widespread. We're still in the early days of people using Internet devices and mobile devices to form social groups."

PART TWO

Primal Perfect

3. The Primal Product or Service

Like genetic code, the primal code is simple yet omnipotent. It unlocks the pattern for creating cultural belief systems and allows leaders the opportunity to implement cues we seek as human beings that help us feel we belong.

Take Starbucks, for example. The creation story is about an enterprising young man who named his Seattle coffee shop after a character in Melville's novel *Moby Dick*. The original creed for Starbucks was that it was a place where people could congregate comfortably, wear berets, smoke clove cigarettes, and discuss Sartre. Today, Starbucks talks about being the "third place"—the other two places being your home and your work. (And look forward to a *fourth* place—your car.) Starbucks icons are that white paper cup you can spot from across the street, the corrugated comfort ring, the green mermaid logo. (Even the higher price can also be viewed as iconic.) Coffee is highly ritualized to begin with, and at Starbucks the caffeinated ritual of affordable luxury is intensified: We stand in line to order our coffee, we stand in another line to get our latte, and then we stand again at the minibar to put in our Nutrasweet and grab a napkin. Pagans? Instant Maxwell House and people who drink Coke for breakfast (or, if you're under thirty, Mountain Dew). Anyone who wants to order at Starbucks first had to learn the sacred words. Whether you're ordering a "venti" coffee, or an "iced grande decaf nonfat latte" you know that it only seems that you're paying by the syllable. And the leader, of course, is Howard Schultz.

Nike's creation story is about how partner Bill Bowerman used a waffle iron in his kitchen to create Nike's original "waffle" sole. Whether you feel Nike is about performance, personal commitment, or unbridled competition, their credo of personal empowerment has resonated for millions of sports enthusiasts and armchair fans alike. Nike's icons begin with their famous swoosh logo but also include sports celebrities like Michael Jordan and Tiger Woods, and the other icons of individual achievement Nike has signed in virtually every sports category. Nike shoes are also iconic. Jocks admit that other footgear may be more comfortable or more functional, but iconic Nike wear just "looks cooler." Sports, as a category, is highly ritualistic: the race, the game, the run, the warm-up stretches, and lacing up the shoes are all a part of the rite of sport. Breaking in Nikes is also an important ritual for athletes, whose feet are an important tool necessary for winning. Pagans in the Nike arena would be Adidas, Puma, and other competing shoe lines. Other nonbelievers would be people who simply don't care about sports. Sacred words that surround Nike include "Waffle," "Air," "Jordan," "Nike Vision," "NikeLab," and other coined phrases. Of course, the most famous set of sacred words in the Nike vocabulary would be "Just do it." The leader, whose vision and passion have guided Nike to world dominance, is Phil Knight.

For generations, the feminine-shaped bottle of Coca-Cola has refreshed people around the globe. The ur-legend of Coke begins in 1886 when a pharmacist in Atlanta named Dr. John Pemberton concocted a soft drink syrup to satisfy drugstore fountain customers. Pemberton gradually sold his ownership interest and died without realizing the potential of the syrup he had created. The cola creed has evolved over the years around the notion of refreshment. Today, the Coca-Cola Company promises to "benefit and refresh everyone it touches." Consumers, however, may be more familiar with slogans that sum up what Coke means to them, like its earliest "Thirst knows no season" in the 1920s, or "It's the real thing" or "Coke is it."

Coke icons include the distinctive contour Coke bottle created in 1915, the red and white Coke ribbon, the famous Coca-Cola Santa (which invented our popular notion of jolly Santa Claus), the animated polar bears featured in Coke Super Bowl advertising, even the six-pack of bottles that Coke innovated. Coca-Cola has become legendary in the world of collectibles, where Coke icons abound. From serving trays to bottle openers, collectors relish Coke icons. Some icons they cannot collect, however, include the iconic shot of Coke being poured into a glass, or the equally classic shot of the sweating youth chugging down a frosty bottle of Coke.

Plenty of rituals surround Coke, including the special family moments, parties, the classic sweaty Coke chug—now an advertising cliché. Tapping the top of the can before opening (to prevent it from spraying), plus including Coke with other flavors like cherry, vanilla, or rum, are other ritual behaviors that surround the Coke brand. Sacred words in the

Coke lexicon include the truncated "Coke" rather than Coca-Cola, "Cherry Coke"; "Diet Coke"; "rum and Coke"; "It's the real thing"; "Coke is it," and their most recent advertising theme, "Make it real."

Pepsi tops the list of Coke pagans. Other nonbelievers would be people who would rather drink milk or water—or any other uncola. Leaders include founder Dr. Pemberton and those who took his invention and with vision and foresight created the Coca-Cola Company we know today, like Asa G. Candler, Robert Woodruff, Sergio Zyman, and current chairman of the board E. Neville Isdell. The result of having all the pieces of primal code in place has been the evolution of one of the world's most beloved and successful brands.

The history of IBM has been one of change and evolution. Originally an office equipment company, in the 1950s Tom Watson, Jr., started the company on a path toward information technologies. The story starts with keypunching information onto cards that were fed into computing machines and stored on magnetic tape. Those machines calculated and compiled and grew into bigger machines. Inside large clean rooms the IBM machines whirred and blinked like a scene out of *Dr. Strangelove.*

The creed at IBM was the famous "Think" slogan posted throughout headquarters and around the world. Years later, threatened by Oracle, Microsoft, Andersen Consulting, Dell, and others, Louis W. Gerstner pursued a coined credo called "e-business." IBM was famous for its army of iconic blue-suited salesmen. The floor-to-ceiling computers of the 1950s were as iconic as the sleek, sexy black box servers of today. A driven sales organization, IBM client meetings were demanding rituals that could make or break a career. Technology is filled with specialized words, from "server" to "MS-DOS". But the sacred words that defined the spirit of the organization were "Think" and "e-business." The leaders of IBM started with Tom Watson, Sr., then Tom Watson, Jr., and extend through Louis W. Gerstner to Sam Palmisano today.

By the 1980s, IBM was a monolith. They seemed impenetrable. The phrase "Nobody ever got fired for buying IBM" reflected IBM's giant presence in the market. But the rise of personal computing and Silicon Valley blindsided the aging giant. Suddenly, sexier and more affordable technologies were pouring onto the market that easily replaced the cumbersome IBM products. I remember walking up to the front desk at IBM corporate headquarters for a meeting. The person behind the reception counter asked who I was visiting and I told him. Unsure of which of the five I.M. Pei–designed buildings my client was quartered in, the guard ignored the IBM computer in front of him and started paging through printed building directories. After a few minutes of watching him fumble through the pages, I asked why he didn't just look on the computer. "Oh, that thing doesn't work," he replied.

At another meeting, I sat in a conference room as the head managers of the IBM Personal Products Division were about to brief the newly appointed president of the division. Before the meeting, the first person to present tried to set up his IBM Thinkpad laptop to show his PowerPoint presentation, but the Thinkpad didn't interface with the projector. One by one, IBM executive vice presidents and vice presidents pulled IBM laptops from their own black computer cases. Not one worked; the presentation was given on an overhead projector.

Just at the moment computing was reaching its zenith and Big Blue should be reaping its rewards, the company was finding itself facing competitive new operating systems, inexpensive personal computers, and hi-tech consulting services.

Worse, people *were* getting fired for buying IBM.

Besieged on all sides, CEO Louis W. Gerstner rallied. There was buzz in the press about something called "e-business." Gerstner seized the notion and made it the company's own. IBM had no more credence for the notion than any other company, except that after fifty years in the marketplace every company had an IBM server buried somewhere in its system with stored data that would keep the new e-world whirring.

IBM also softened its Big Blue public image in the face of the soft-clad, business-casual Silicon Valley folks. Its agency, Ogilvy, hired the same people who created the Apple advertising. Soon, the image of IBM Corporation turned from oversized, uncaring, and monolithic to empathetic problem solvers providing intelligent solutions to complex business problems. IBM television commercials, with their film festival blue bands top and bottom, became the envy of every other advertiser. Every time an IBM television commercial came on the air, everyone knew who was advertising.

By adjusting the creed, icons, and rituals of the company (as well as its product and service offerings) IBM reshaped itself to fit the evolving world. Today, nobody's getting fired for buying IBM any more.

* * *

In the late 1990s it seemed that every article that talked about the fledgling amazon.com talked about how founder Jeff Bezos and his wife drove cross-country to California to get its initial funding. As his wife drove, Jeff sat in the backseat and wrote amazon's business plan. A wonderful creation story. Following the crash of the dot-coms the creed at amazon.com matured. It is no longer just about making product lines "as wide as the Amazon" available for sale over the Internet, but has rebooted itself to become the earth's "most consumer centric company." Icons for the amazon brand include the familiar amazon.com Web page itself, the amazon.com logo, and the smiling amazon package delivered to your door. Amazon.com rituals are all about logging on, searching for products, and the purchase. Customers are invited to write their own book reviews. The arrival of their purchase a few days later is another welcome amazon ritual. Pagans for amazon.com include bricks and mortar stores and people who don't shop online. The sacred words are the reviews and lists of recommended books and music, even the personalization. The leader is Jeff Bezos.

Mass ideologies also fall under the primal branding construct. Consider democracy, American-style. The creation story of how our founding fathers were tired of taxation without representation is a tale heard since grade school. The creed? All men are created equal. Our rituals as American citizens are extensive (the longer an ideology has been in place, the longer its primal list) and include voting, raising the flag, lowering it to half-mast, the Fourth of July, Thanksgiving, Memorial Day, reciting the Pledge of Allegiance, and more. Images such as the flag, the Washington Monument,

Mount Rushmore, the Lincoln Memorial, and the White House are indelible icons of American democracy. The melodies of "The Star Spangled Banner" and "America, the Beautiful" have also become iconic sound effects of life as American citizens. Our pagans have always been well known, starting with British redcoats during the foundation of our democracy. Over the years, we have battled Nazis, communists, totalitarianism, and most recently, terrorists. The sacred words? *E pluribus unum,* "In God we trust," "We the people," "Yankee," and more. Our leaders include every president since George Washington.

This cry for freedom would later come from France and the same primal construct would be in play. Instead of freedom, they would cry for *liberté.* And instead of rituals like riding Tories on rails, or tar-and-feathering, they substituted the deadly rite of the French guillotine. Other social ideologies like communism, Nazism, the ecology, civil rights, women's, and antiwar movements can also be deconstructed into their primal elements.

Primal branding also helps to explain pop-up ideologies: those instant successes that seemingly pop out of nowhere and inexplicably find eager masses. Low-carb diets, Harry Potter, Nascar, wrestling, the World Poker Tour. Even political candidates have a primal explanation for their popularity.

Take the low-carb craze, for example. The creation story is a fizzy blend of the popular Dr. Atkins and South Beach diets. The creed is how eating less carbohydrates leads to a more fit and, consequently, more attractive life. The icons are the flat stomachs and happy smiles of low-carb models. The pagans, of course, are high carbs and overweight people. Rituals are the daily consumption of low-carb foods, low-carb shopping experiences, and the low-carb buzz on the media, at work, in the gym, and with friends. The sacred words are the invented lexicon of low-carb products, including Atkins, South Beach, Sugar Busters, the Zone, Carbohydrate Addicts, and Protein Power. The leaders are Dr. Atkins and other low-carb advocates.

You can even explain the long-standing popularity of *Gilligan's Island* (and *Star Trek* and *The Sopranos*) thanks to its primal aspects. If you're unclear about Gilligan's creation story, listen to the song lyrics that kick off each episode. Every show has the same creed: Get off the island. The ritual that faces the cast each episode is how they are going to attempt to get off the island (and their ritual failure), the Howells' afternoon cocktail, and Professor's mechanical wizardry. The icons include the ship, the island, Gilligan's hat, and more. In fact, over time each and every character on the show has become iconic (who would you rather marry— Ginger or Mary Ann?). The pagans are anyone not shipwrecked on the island and people who watch *Survivor*. The leader is not Gilligan after all, but Skipper. To spur your own thinking you might try outlining the seven pieces of primal code for *Star Wars* or *Star Trek* on your own.

Primal branding is a powerful tool to help create, manage, propel, and motivate successful brands. However, look at products and services like BankOne, Lestoil, Goodrich, MCI, Kia, Qwest, Xcel Energy, Micron. They may be successful businesses, certainly, but they are built along functional attribute lines. It would be difficult to describe where they are from, what they believe, their actions, language, or who leads them. Even the company logos escape us. More-over, as soon as another product comes along that is faster, better, cheaper, or more powerful, they will be particularly vulnerable to the whims of fickle consumers. (Anyone who looks at Xcel Energy, a regional energy monopoly and says, "Why should a monopoly care?" should remember that AT&T was once an anonymous monopoly, too.)

It is important to note that while brands that engage all seven pieces of code become the most successful and resonate with the greatest public appeal, companies in some latent categories can beat their competition by engaging just a few pieces of code. Categories like banking and finance, telecommunications, utilities, and health care (and others) have been underwhelming their publics for years. By activating and communicating just a few pieces of code in meaningful ways, companies can create a tactile bond with their consumer base that would help differentiate them, create consumer preference, and deepen customer relationships. This could have dramatic effects in brand value and financial performance.

How to find Cyan Worlds headquarters is as much of a mystery as wandering through the labyrinth worlds of Cyan's blockbuster gaming hits Myst, Riven, and Uru. There is no oversized sign boasting the presence of this multimillion-dollar corporation. Except for the security gate, the road to the headquarters building outside Spokane, Washington, looks like an entrance to any of the trailer parks along the highway. (The underwhelming entrance, one later learns, is to deter gawkers and overzealous game enthusiasts.)

A code is punched into the keypad and the gate crawls

sideways. Obelisks of basalt stand like sentinels in the shade of jack pines. Two low buildings lay on opposite sides of the parking lot. Visitors cross a short wooden bridge to enter the headquarters building, as if crossing into one of Cyan's computer-enhanced worlds. The Cyan Worlds headquarters is an homage to the foggy, terrestrial mindscape of Myst that Rand and Robin Miller created back in 1987. The interior is styled in organic shapes of wood and steel, an aesthetic familiar to the millions of Myst and Riven enthusiasts around the world. Two copies of the Myst book in hardcover lie on top of the reception desk, with yellow stickies asking that they be personalized and signed.

The company started in the late 1980s, when two brothers, Rand and Ryan Miller, were creating educational games. They designed a game called Manhole, one of the first games to be designed for a new computer medium called the CD-ROM. In 1991, they received funding to develop a new game, code-named "Myst." Working from their homes the game took five people two years and over twenty thousand man hours to develop. "Myst was a project that we were just excited about, and you know, it felt like it was on the edge," says CEO Rand Miller. "There was a heck of a lot of work. We weren't sure we would be able to do it, but none of that mattered. It was cool."

Myst was markedly different from the stealth-and-stalk games that other developers were creating, like Mortal Kombat, Tank, and Doom. "I see a lot of hotshot groups right out of college who just need ten million dollars," says Doug Carlston, former CEO of Broderbund, the company that first financed and distributed Myst. "A lot of their work has a kind of sameness to it, the stuff they played when they were teenagers. I got the sense when I saw Myst, it was nothing I had ever seen before. That's what Broderbund was looking for." Instead of blasting away with plasma cannons at undefeatable cyberforces, players of Myst found themselves engaged in a complex narrative. They used their brains instead of their thumbs to grope through a puzzling landscape that was somehow organic and affirming. Myst was to Mortal Kombat what Bob Dylan is to Ramstein.

"We thought differently," says Rand Miller. "It's like, Why do we die in these games? Why can something kill you and you have to start over? Why don't we weave a story into it, where I find myself in the middle of something? All those things were things that we didn't research," adds Miller. "We just liked them."

"They recognized that if something was good, it almost didn't matter what the technical force behind it was," adds Doug Carlston. "Myst began as a piece of paper that Rand played with his church group. Later, Rand turned it into a hypercard stack." Their sense of being different made a difference. Myst and its sequel, Riven, have sold over 12 million units worldwide, becoming some of the best-selling computer games in history.

In the beginning, Rand and Ryan worked at home. They held meetings in a garage outfitted with office cubes. Today, nearly fifty developers, artists, musicians, assistants, computer geeks, and gaming nerds wander the halls of Cyan Worlds. Iconic artifacts from the worlds of Myst, Riven, and Uru are everywhere. Two full-sized costumes created as models for Riven hang in Plexiglas display cases in the entryway. Character studies hang on office walls. A clay model from one of the game environments sits in a hallway: mountainous spires carved from gray clay, village habitats in red clay. Workstations are not called office cubes but pods, and combine elements of steel and Northwestern pine, giving the environment a Hobbit-meets-Silicon-Spokane feel.

In one pod, a designer clicks through one prototype scenario after another. A figure walks through an environment of mushroomlike nodes. Spores drift through the air like snowflakes. Computer code runs in a corner of the screen as the designer's fingers tap at the keyboard. In another room lights have been dimmed. Overhead, a black oval semisphere hangs above the work pods; pinholes of illumination prick the darkness. Enthusiasts would recognize this as the Stardome from Riven.

When projects are in full swing employees become a tightly knit team working 24/7 on deadline. To keep the organization intimate, Miller tries to keep the numbers small.

"I think we've had a little over fifty people," he says. "But then things start to change. You start relying more on the attitude of those lower in the rank to set the tone, and that can be good and that can be bad. From the CEO perspective, you really lose the personal touch, which I think is one of our benefits."

Decisions are made quickly in order to meet deadlines and keep the digital narrative vibrant. A misstep anywhere along the line can lead to expensive redos that become time-sucking creative sinkholes, moments of lost momentum and enthusiasm drain pools. Communication is key. "That's all this is about, frankly, is communication," says Miller. "Any person who's working on the production on some particular item they don't know about has the freedom to come to any person on the design team and say, What did you mean by this? or, Hey, I have an idea that fits with this. And that happens on a regular basis. That goes for me as well. I mean, my office is open to anyone who wants to come in and say those things as well. From, Here's an idea I have for the company, or, Here's an idea I have for the game, or, Here's a problem I see. That happens every day."

While an open-door policy is not news, Cyan's longevity is. A company's lifespan in the duck-and-dodge world of computer gaming can be measured in nanoseconds. Surviving for twenty years is nearly miraculous.

"The industry is just crazy with regard to what's successful and what's not and what's foreseen and what's not, and how much you get back compared to the amount of work and how many hours you put in," sighs Miller. "Just crazy, crazy."

To keep Cyan alive amid the mystic forces of the marketplace, thinking differently has become only a part of the company mantra. There's another way that Miller has tried to boil down the code. "People want to matter," he says. "It's that simple. I mean, especially in our industry, there's everything from, I want to play Shooter, because I can get a better score, to our adventure gaming, which is, I want to matter because I've discovered something, or, I've found this on my own, or, I've found a secret, I wonder if anyone else found this. And, with the online version of our game, we've had a lot of people who would go online just to help other people, trying to satisfy the same desire, Well, I matter if I help somebody."

In the ritualized process of development, like many CEOs running smaller companies, Miller makes himself engaged. More important, he keeps the structure at Cyan relatively unstructured. "The publishers go nuts trying to figure out exactly how the milestones work," says Miller. "But inevitably, we get the job done." Project managers count on the fact that the design is going to change as a part of the production. "We don't lay it in stone," explains Miller. "We pass it on to the next person and just go down the assembly line. They come back and it changes and evolves as part of actually producing it. It's not the most efficient way to do it, but it really gives everybody a feeling like they're having a part of this thing as it moves forward."

Miller tries to integrate fun into the grueling process of game development. "We are probably the only company in the world, that I know of, that has Deviled Egg Wednesday," he laughs. They also have the occasional movie day, when the company is shut down and everyone goes to the movies. Workers roll scooters through the aisles. Miller leans over and peers out his office. "This time of year we give everyone Christmas lights; there's some very creative stringing up." Some clusters look as if they've been grabbed from the pack and thrown against the wall. Others are strung merrily around the pod. Visitors are reminded that these people have been hired for their imagination.

When his brother, Ryan, left the company a few years ago to pursue other interests, Rand also thought about pulling back. He tried to be less hands-on and started to insert competent managers in key production roles. "That didn't work at all," declares a low-key Miller. After a few years of coming in and out of the production process at will, Miller realized that line people were confused about who was in charge and frustrated about sudden changes in direction. Worse, ranking managers felt they were being second-guessed. What was merely frustration for Miller was pandemonium for those working under him. After a few years of trying to work textbook-style, Miller decided that leadership needed to be clear.

"We went back to the way we like doing it and everybody breathed a sigh of relief," declares Miller. "It feels good again now. Once we changed back, motivation levels went up. Even though it's not always easy, it feels like it's a good place to work, people enjoy it."

Cyan consciously reinforces the opinions of their fan base, the core believers who believe in them most. "We go to an awful lot of effort," says Miller. They hold special events for fans. One of the events was a cryptic Web-based treasure hunt that was never publicized or open to the masses. Only insider brand evangelists knew about it. It didn't even have a name. "It was a closely held, fan-based thing that was incredibly work-intensive for us," says Miller. "I mean, people traveled to different parts of the country, sat in front of phone booths at particular times, and got phone calls from people. And every day there was new information posted on the Web, and it lasted for months and months. It was just a small group of people that took part in that, it was a blast for us to do, and it made the fans happy."

Some corporations view their followers from a distance,

but Cyan keeps in touch with them on a daily basis. "We actually have a person on staff who attempts to answer every e-mail that we get by hand," says Miller. "We keep up on the pulse. And there are friendships, on top of everything else." Cyan's commitment to the people who engage in their imaginary worlds is real. "We feel like those people contribute to us, the least we can do is to pass a little bit back. And they've been incredibly loyal."

The Miller brothers began the saga of Cyan Worlds with their breakthrough Manhole CD-ROM, then went on to create blockbuster Myst. Their creed has evolved from the obligatory "creating the best games ever," to a more transcendent, "I matter." The icons for Cyan Worlds rise from the games—the pods and citadels and peaceful gardens from imaginary worlds that the employees create themselves. Some of the rituals in the 24/7 world of game development are also play-based: a Frisbee court, hanging Christmas tree lights in free-form expression. Other rituals like the Web-based treasure hunt are invented for ardent fans. The informal management style and constant communicating of valuable processes are also ritualized events. Within the garage mentality of Cyan the pagans are corporate madness at some level and all the assault and victory games like Ever Quest and Marathon at another. Cyan Worlds has created its own set of sacred words, Myst, Riven, Uru, and more. The leader, of course, is Rand Miller. But the real leaders are the people who play Myst and the other games. Whether they play for fun or for mastery, they play in order to belong to a world that shimmers with primal code. "In the end," concludes Miller, "I matter. If I belong to something, I matter.

And you're either going to belong to something that has some substance, or you're going to belong to something that perhaps doesn't have as much substance. Like Coke."

A movie is playing. In the darkness, an audience sits and watches, eyes intent on the screen. George C. Scott playing General George S. Patton strides onto the stage, a supersized American flag behind him. It is the opening scene of the movie *Patton*. As Patton delivers his famous speech, someone has dubbed in new words. Instead of saying "fucking Germans," the voice says "fucking *Fortune,*" as in the magazine. The audience giggles.

Another line, another laugh. The response is predictable, nearly staged. After all, the audience is not a cross section of middle America moviegoers but the writers and creators of *Fast Company,* the magazine that has vowed to give business journalism a kick in the ass. The story starts when Alan Webber was given a fellowship by the Japan Society of New York to spend three months in Japan. His mission? To visit that country and see what was going on. Back in 1989, there was a lot going on. This was at the height of the Japanese bubble, in a world before flip phones, personal digital assistants, laptop computers, digital cameras, or even the Internet (back in the states, Milli Vanilli, New Kids On the Block, and Debbie Gibson were hanging on the charts). In fact, for the young editor from *Harvard Business Review* the disparity between the United States and Japan made Webber's experience more like an awakening than a sabbatical. "I had a phenomenal three-month experience over there as a person interested in what was going to change in the future of Japan and where new ideas were coming from," says Webber from his home today in Santa Fe. In trips to digital research labs and through Japanese stores Webber found himself being ushered into the future. He came back to Boston and the *Harvard Business Review* with fresh insights that would shape his own future.

"One was that technology was going to change the world," outlines Webber. "Second was the ongoing evolution of the global economy. Third was a generational changing of the guard." His experience would put him at odds with the ivy-covered institution that employed him. Webber sensed a new world emerging, and it was neither stuffy nor conservative nor especially white. "I noticed coming back to *Harvard Business Review*," recounts Webber, "and seeing the composition of the incoming class of Harvard Business School MBA candidates. It was just a massive influx of diversity. And the old network of white men in business running everything, those days were seriously numbered."

Webber felt the disconnect between what he had seen in Japan, and the way that the *Harvard Business Review* and other U.S. business magazines like *Fortune, Forbes,* and *Business Week* wrote about dynamism and change. He shared his thoughts with one of the brightest editors of the review, a fellow named Bill Taylor. "We were seeing something very different from what most business magazines were writing about," says Webber. And they realized they couldn't turn the *HBR* into that vehicle. "If we were ever going to try something on our own and make a run for a magazine that we invented and we had equity in and we could shape from the beginning, the time was right," says Webber.

Over the course of several months Webber and Taylor located funding from sources in Japan, Canada, and the United States. But they approached their investors for more than just cash. "We wanted people who were brand names themselves in the world of business, who brought credibility, who brought their own ideas and intelligence about the world and the world of business. And we wanted their Rolodexes. We wanted to use their connections to get deeper into the community of business leaders we thought needed to be written about."

The inaugural issue of *Fast Company* popped up on the newsstands in November 1995. Shouting THE NEW RULES OF BUSINESS, it outlined the mantras that would make it famous: "Work is personal"; "Computing is social"; "Knowledge is Power"; "Break the rules." Readers discovered that the way the editors talked about business was as feisty as the entrepreneurs and business leaders they wrote about. In contrast to the stuffed-armchair quality of the *Harvard Business Review,* Webber and Taylor found a snappy voice that was part business, part bravado. "We described the magazine initially as a cross between *Harvard Business Review* and *Rolling Stone,*" explains Webber. "We clearly were targeting a much more lively, creative audience. We wanted to be a magazine that appealed to people who were interested in change and innovation. And who thought, as we did, that the world was on the cusp of a major transformation. And they wanted to be a part of it, rather than a victim of it."

The editors of *Fast Company* encouraged their writers to create a new lexicon for the new economy springing up in Silicon Valley, Silicon Alley, and the Pacific Rim. If they did not create words and phrases such as "outsourcing," "change agent," and "fire starter," the magazine served as cultural potting soil for them to take root and grow.

Fast Company did more than simply report what was going on; it often seemed that it *was* what was going on. It challenged the 24/7/365 work ethic and encouraged readers to think better, deeper, faster than those in the cubicles next door. The editors made it a point to publish about people before they were famous, and publish about ideas before they were safe. They found the most interesting and cutting-edge experiments and practices that people were exploring and reported on them before they had a chance to shake up the status quo.

"We got a pretty positive reaction from readers and advertisers alike," says Webber. "We ended up doing what successful magazines always do. We created a community."

Fast Company transitioned from being more than a transaction; the new magazine became a relationship. They found a group who shared the magazine's values and believed in what the magazine had to offer. "One of the things I thought was wonderful about *Fast Company,*" says Webber, "is that we ended up with something called the Company of Friends, almost growing spontaneously from the readership. People wanted to know who else was in their community, their city. Who was a leader of the magazine that they could connect with—and network with. We ended up with the Chamber of Commerce of the Future spread all over the world, with chapters in Paris and Tokyo, São Paolo, as well as all over the United States." These de facto groups were self-organizing and communicated through the *Fast Company* Web site and e-mail. They communicated their excitement about the world of work as a positive, enhanced experience. A place where individuals had more to say about how the world of work operated.

Almost from the beginning *Fast Company* printed the iconic e-mail address of the author and the people who were in the story. They sponsored and enabled communication from all parties, weaving together their own vast network, encouraging conversation and involvement between members of the *Fast Company* community. "Readers became more than just readers," says Webber. "They became fans and people invested in the magazine's future."

There was also a community fast developing inside the *Fast Company* offices. Webber and Taylor tore down the imagined Chinese wall that existed between editorial and advertisers. Advertisers, after all, were often some of the companies leading the charge into the new economy. The leaders also decided they would remove any barriers between other parts of the magazine. The Web site, the magazine editorial staff, and the newly instituted conference business were all interlocking pieces of the same business organization. Everything was fluid, flexible, and motivated forward.

Even the office design promoted interaction. In the beginning, office space was minimal so interaction was natural. As the magazine grew the staff grew, and so did the office space. They established a kitchen area, nicknamed "the boomerang," as the communal center. In the boomerang, staffers could stop and chat with one another and discover what was going on in other parts of the magazine—and the world.

"There was a sense of informality," says Webber. There

was also a sense of urgency. "We weren't all sweetness and light," Webber admits. "A part of the culture was sink or swim. People worked hard; we had very high standards. The expectations were tough in terms of how good you were going to be at what you did. We didn't suffer fools gladly. Happily, we didn't make very many hiring mistakes. But I think for a number of people who joined up there was a moment of truth where they either said, 'O.K. I get it, I can play this game,' or they just got thrown off by the sink or swim nature of life at *Fast Company*."

The typically fast, fluid nature of running the magazine reflected the by-the-nanosecond business culture they felt themselves a part of. Instead of the four-box matrixes of *Harvard Business Review* or the reports and profiles of other magazines *Fast Company* was the vernacular of smart business conversation, the voice of innovation and creativity.

"We really wanted to have an intelligent conversation with the reader," says Webber. "What we told all of our employees at *Fast Company,* we were doing a magazine that helped decode what worked and didn't work in the world of business. We weren't reporting just for news value. We were trying to decode the operating principles underneath a company's success, behind a person's leadership style, involved in a company's approach to innovation or creativity. And suss out the thematic crosscuts that really would be useful and instructional to our readers."

Webber describes the magazine as being in the "edutainment" business. "We were trying to educate the reader," says Webber. "But I had learned from the *HBR* that if you make the education too bland, nobody wants to swallow it." Webber adds, "*HBR* was like a bran muffin. It was good for you, but it wasn't very appetizing." *Fast Company* became the bible for a new generation of businesspeople of all ages, industries, and styles. The magazine had a snap-and-crackle vocabulary better suited to the digital information age and entrepreneurs discovering billion-dollar businesses in their dorm rooms. The *Fast Company* style was fast-paced, articulate, inventive, and successful. The staff grew from seven people to seventy. And while the founders did not measure success by their circulation numbers, those also grew.

"What's your definition of victory?" Webber poses the question. "We looked at things like e-mail traffic, reports from people that they tore out *Fast Company* pages and put them up in their cubicles. Companies e-mailing other companies that were written about in our magazine. We were looking for impact, not just dollars and cents and pure growth for growth's sake." He pauses. "As it turns out, you can do both."

The story of how *Fast Company* was created by two editors with already successful careers (Bill Taylor had already worked with Ralph Nader and run *Sloan Management Review* before joining *Harvard Business Review*) who jumped ship to create something new mirrored the stories of the people they wrote about. In doing so, they styled their creed around new business journalism, a.k.a. "not your father's business magazine." It was not a step they took lightly. After all, as Webber admits, "ninety percent of all magazines starting out fail in their first year."

The icons were the issues of *Fast Company* that appeared on newsstands each month. This was a monthly ritual for an eager, appreciative audience. And its arrival sparked other rituals, like e-mailing between companies, employees, and subscribers. *Fast Company*'s conference business became another ritual and, as long as the companies out there had the funding, it was a business unto itself. Other rituals sprang up inside the *Fast Company* organization itself. Simple stuff like movie night. Good coffee (Webber claims that while an army runs on its stomach, a magazine runs on its coffee). Hallway chat. Hello parties for new employees, good-bye parties for exiting ones. Today, there is even a loose-knit *Fast Company* alumni association that meets semiregularly in Manhattan.

The sacred words of the primal code were the crisp new biz speak greeted by enthusiastic readers. As the writers of *Fast Company* wrote about "free agents" and "thought leaders" they propelled a new vocabulary for the new economy they believed themselves to be a part of. The magazine was also the first to break concepts like Tom Peters's "the brand called you."

Those who did not believe in *Fast Company* were likely to be people tied to the old technologies. Pagans were pretty easy to find. After all, what were the differences between *Harvard Business Review* and *Fast Company*? "Everything," exclaims Alan Webber. The leaders of *Fast Company* were able to build a community of businesspeople who got it; they sought out and supported each other over the Internet and at *Fast Company* conventions. Today, that community continues to grow and evolve. Some of the companies *Fast Company* wrote about are now gone, or have been reshaped to fit the new economy after 9/11. Others still thrive.

After seven years of magazine reinvention, and as their publisher sought out a buyer for the magazine, Webber and

Taylor decided it was time to create an exit strategy. Ultimately, they decided to go out the same way they came in. When they sold their stake in the magazine they gave everyone a stake. Webber explains, "We put into the sales agreement that there would be a pot of money created by the purchasers, so that the employees got a taste of the sale."

They had blazingly good jobs. They could have stayed where they were and led happy, complacent lives. But having revealed the new, they could not return to the old ways. The success of Alan Webber and Bill Taylor is much like the success of those they wrote about. Inspired. Gutsy. Innovative. Smart. They saw an old world grinding down and a shiny new order emerging. They took a step into the void and found a rising escalator step carrying them toward a distant star. And they left behind a bright new world for others to wake up in.

Lessons learned? At first, Webber's answer sounds as if it comes off an inspiration poster. "If you don't do it, then you fail absolutely," he quips. "If you do it and you fail, at least you've taken a shot at it." Okaaay. Then Webber pauses, remembers something. "I got an e-mail about a month ago from a woman who said, I just wanted to tell you *Fast Company* meant a huge amount to my life and made a huge difference." Webber takes a breath. "That seems to me to be a pretty good obituary."

A shipment of yellow roses from Costa Rica is delivered to a Manhattan flower shop. A housewife signs for a dress she bought the day before off the Internet. A transmission assembly arrives at an automobile manufacturing plant just in time to be bolted into place. Our world is pieced together by a shadow network of supply and demand that is held in synchronous motion thanks to the dream of a teenaged bike messenger a hundred years ago who started the largest logistics and delivery company in the world. UPS founder Jim Casey (company myth suggests he might have been only thirteen) pooled together one hundred dollars from friends to open a bike messenger service in Seattle called American Messenger Company. Starting on August 28, 1907, Jim Casey and his friends delivered messages, packages, and pitchers of beer around Seattle. That was his humble opening as a pioneer in the delivery business.

"The innovation that got the company started was the consolidation of packages," says Larry Bloomenkranz, vice president of global brand management and advertising. In a time when few people owned their own automobile, department stores had expensive vehicle fleets to deliver customer's purchases. "Jim's big idea was [that] rather than having each department store run their own fleet, if he could get the contract from four or five different department stores to make deliveries, he could do it a lot more efficiently." Casey demonstrated that he could do the delivery drop cheaper than department stores could do themselves. "The idea of consolidating deliveries and pickups and putting them into a preexisting system was how the company got its beginning," says Bloomenkranz, "It was really the first hub-and-spoke."

Jim Casey constantly innovated. He invented the world's first package-sorting machine. He created the world's first air express service. As his business spread beyond Seattle and he opened operations in Oakland, California, Casey changed the name of the company to United Parcel Service (UPS). Twenty years after he opened his doors, three New York retailers turned their delivery business over to UPS and the company became national, expanding operations throughout the East and the Midwest.

Today, UPS enables global commerce through supply chain management, package and document delivery, financing, and other services. With over 3.6 billion packages and documents annually, UPS delivers to every address in North America and Europe and to two hundred countries and territories. It is the eleventh largest airline in the world, with over two thousand flights each day.

For all its dimension and scope today, UPS still operates under principles founded by Jim Casey. "He was a simple and humble guy," says Larry Bloomenkranz, "but he was also a visionary in the sense that he was attuned to developments in the world in terms of technology, and also what's the right way to treat a workforce."

The combination of advanced technology and personal humility are principles that continue to drive the entire UPS organization. Everyone is called by their first name, from CEO to truck washer. People are promoted from within. Many of the top managers started as drivers and package sorters. The humble brown vehicles are another egalitarian expression of the company. Instead of being boastful rolling billboards, they are simple brown boxes that blend into the urban landscape. "We didn't want to impose our name and color on our customers," says Bloomenkranz. The idea was that the company was merely an intermediary. "It was by design an understated appearance," says Bloomenkranz. Jim

Casey's credo was "We represent our customers, not ourselves."

To many visitors, a UPS distribution center seems like a Willy Wonka factory designed by Rube Goldberg. Endless conveyor belts and package expressways loop around the vast industrial warehouse like a flattened-out roller coaster. It is mid-afternoon and the conveyors are semiretired, waiting for the trucks to return, a perfect time for visitors. In the evening and morning as trucks purr at the loading dock, the area is elbow to elbow with people and packages. Lasers scan tracking bar codes at dozens per second, and the packages are routed, separated, loaded, and sped away in a manner that is part pandemonium, part routine. Underneath all the purposeful frenzy lies a bedrock of belief that permeates the entire organization. The egalitarian nature of the company is a working mechanism that promotes camaraderie and community, driven by a strong creed.

"Our policy book is a series of statements about what we believe in," says Larry Bloomenkranz. "It covers everything from the way we pay our suppliers on a timely basis to how we manage our reputation to how we treat our customers in a certain way. It's about fifty pages, and it lays out the policies and beliefs of the company." While this might sound de rigueur (what organization doesn't have a tome that the human relations department hands to new employees), the difference at UPS is that their policies are continually in use and kept fresh. "The policy book is something that is constantly used and referred to at meetings and at conferences," says Bloomenkranz. "It's a living document that's on everybody's shelf."

In the 1930s, all of this happened on a much simpler scale. Even then, Jim Casey was thinking about how to get people to behave in a positive way that would portray the values of his organization. Then he had an idea. "The idea of employee ownership was, at that time, a revolutionary concept," says Larry Bloomenkranz. United Parcel Service parceled out to managers what they called "brown shares." "Jim Casey understood human emotional needs and said, This is how you treat people right so they'll do the best for our company. His management style was very direct, very respectful and egalitarian. That was also one of the things that lead to the cohesive brand experience that people have with this company."

Another piece of the UPS creed runs according to the strictest principles of time management. The precise delivery of packages, documents, financing, and other resources is a synchronous melding of man, machines, and meteorology. UPS owns one of the largest information technology networks on the planet. It is able to track each package from pickup to delivery, from Beijing to Boston and back. UPS is the largest force in the new supply-on-demand economy, and that role is growing.

Brown is beautiful. Over 88,000 brown-painted UPS trucks and vehicles deliver to nearly 8 million retail stores, manufacturing plants, corporations, and homes each business day. The iconic color brown has been with the company since the early 1920s, when it was known as "Pullman brown," the color of the deluxe Pullman Palace Car Company and its first-class train cars. The familiar brown delivery vehicles can be spotted behind malls, in alleys, and double-parked on Manhattan side streets. The UPS driver clad in brown shorts is another icon. The handheld bar code scanner is an icon, and so is the UPS label. The brown box rolled in on the two-wheeler is also a strong icon, although during the 2003 global rebranding effort (the fourth in the company's ninety-eight-year history) the package became a liability.

"The package on the top with the little string on it is where we're from," says Larry Bloomenkranz. "But it's not the strongest representation of where this company is going in the future." Design firm FutureBrand developed a new corporate logo sans box in keeping with today's supply chain economy. In a move similar to when United Parcel Service officially became UPS, the new logo mark reflects the company's package service heritage, but allows room for a business unit like UPS Capital, which provides financing arrangements and loans for small businesses, to also flourish.

"Our business strategy was very much about evolutionary change and growing into these other capability areas," says Bloomenkranz. "We want to make sure that our visual identity reflects that business strategy throughout. Therefore, the shield you see today is different enough to be noticeable, but not a brand-new thing you wouldn't recognize."

The UPS Store has become another icon in strip malls and retail locations throughout the country. That number was increased when UPS acquired the Mail Boxes, Etc., chain with its additional fifteen hundred stores.

The comings and goings of the UPS guy are a welcome ritual at over 6 million retail stores every day. As most ladies know (and anyone who's seen *Legally Blonde*), the brown

Bermuda-clad UPS driver has become a sexy cult figure, an appeal neither endorsed nor promoted by UPS. "There was an article written about it in the *Wall Street Journal,* I think," says Steve Holmes, a vice president in the UPS PR department. "Next, a UPS driver was featured as one of the world's sexiest people in *People* magazine. It's something the media got going." There are other reasons people look forward to the arrival of the UPS guy. When the driver shows up with his two-wheeler filled with packages, according to one excited retailer, "It's just like Christmas!"

UPS is such an essential part of our economic bones that when the International Brotherhood of Teamsters held a fifteen-day strike of UPS workers back in 1997, some stores ran out of inventory. UPS management pitched in, resuming their roles as drivers to keep the packages flowing, but with the daily ritual disrupted, client companies suddenly realized their unwitting reliance on UPS. Some even invited competitors to come in and temporarily take up the slack.

Part of the reason UPS is such a welcome ritual is because of rituals that exist inside UPS itself. Each morning, drivers attend a prework communications meeting (PCM). "It's a two- to three-minute meeting where a topic is discussed," says Larry Bloomenkrantz. "It might be something local or something important to the company as a whole. It's a mechanism that happens with all the drivers, at all the centers, every day." As a part of time-management economics UPS has developed time-sensitive behaviors for their drivers that have become ingrained minirituals. Drivers are trained to carry keys on their pinkie finger, so keys are at the ready. The driver puts his seat belt on at the same time he starts the vehi-

cle. They walk at a set pace: two steps per second. This thinking in terms of measurements and methods creates a consistent way of thinking across a company of 384,000 employees.

"In God we trust," winks Steve Holmes. "All other things,
we measure."

And there are other rituals. Filling out the UPS form,
scanning the bar code, signing for the shipment. UPS's egalitarian creed is even played out by mandating that everyone
be referred to on a first-name basis.

Sacred words for UPS include "brown shares," the original UPS employee-owned stock. Operational words like
the "prework communications meeting" and the text of the
policy book are also sacred words. So is the company's
newest mantra, "synchronized commerce" and, of course,
the word immortalized in the latest UPS advertising campaign, "brown." There are also many dozens of revered
words dedicated to the synchronicity of delivering over 14
million pieces each day. They are the argot of inventory
management, commercial finance, supply chains, aeronau-
tics, information technologies, customs clearance, and trade
documentation.

The pagans within UPS are the devils of inefficiency. The
time-sucking distance between two points. The asynchro-
nous pieces of time spent sitting at traffic lights, waiting in
lobbies, or wasting precious nanoseconds for information
data to download.

Although there are many competitors trying to service the
new supply chain economy, no one can really compete with
the long-established size and scope of the UPS infrastructure. Consulting companies like Accenture and IBM and

other delivery companies like FedEx and DHL try to lever-age their specialties to fractionalize UPS's hold. But as one UPS television commercial declared, those companies can't do what they propose, they just propose it. UPS can march its brown-clad army of personnel, vehicles, and airplanes toward any opportunity—and add information technology and millions in financing—and create a win-win.

In fact, it is within the new "make it simple, make it better, make it mine" global supply chain reality where UPS shines best. With global economies moving toward faster cycle times, faster inventory turns, more one-to-one, they favor smaller, more frequent shipments rather than large bulk shipments. "We have seen and been taking advantage of this trend in the United States and see the same trend happening right now as Europe becomes more integrated," says Bloomenkranz. Let's say you're manufacturing goods in China destined for a retailer with stores all over the United States. Rather than the traditional model where goods are put on pallets in China and come across the ocean in containers and get broken down again into pallets in distribution centers, and those pal-lets get broken down to be shipped to individual stores, UPS does it all in one synchronous motion. As goods are made in China they are prelabeled and shipped directly to the retail store, eliminating warehousing time and cost. The advan-tages are clear in terms of inventory, cash flow, and speed to market.

"This drive toward faster movements and smaller units is something that just keeps continuing from manufacturer to final consumer," says Bloomenkranz. The harmonious blend of shipping, financing, and speedy customs clearance, plus the information technologies and personnel that make it all possible is a synchronized effort that only UPS can execute. "It's a very interesting time," understates Bloomenkranz.

UPS is a webbed community of employees, customers, and services held together by a vibrant belief system. Jim Casey's original idea of "managing by the owners and owned by the managers" is still strong. The company culture was, and still is, to create generalists by promoting people to a variety of assignments. As people are blended through the organization, a UPS way of doing things emerges. There are no reserved parking spaces. No one flies first class. Alcohol is forbidden during work hours (not just for drivers but for all employees). In a company filled with industrial engineers there is a consistency of approach and a way of doing things that is passed from one generation to the next. "People know in their gut what the right thing to do is," says Larry Bloomenkranz. "And it's been reinforced throughout a long career and a consistent experience in terms of how people at UPS act and how do they do things. That's one of the strengths of this company."

The strength of the UPS belief system is reinforced by cash. Until 1999, all stock within the company was held by employees. That's been happening since the 1930s. "Everybody who works here has a significant portion of their equity tied up in the company," says Bloomenkranz. "That's another strong element of the brand that makes it a community."

From Jim Casey's teenage dream to Mike Eskew, the current chief executive officer, the story of UPS is one of a strong creed designed around efficiency and quality of service. The signature brown vehicles and uniforms provide an iconic backdrop for the synchronous beat of global supply and demand. The rituals of UPS are ingrained in the steady breathing of daily commerce. Those rituals go from proper routing down to the key on the driver's pinkie finger. The vernacular of commercial shipping, customs, and finance are the sacred words for UPS, while the fiends of inefficiency and time delays—as well as competitor companies—are the pagans. UPS has enabled its drivers and managers to create the most synchronous delivery system on the planet, able to deliver nearly 4 billion packages a year. This is a daily logistics effort infused with a powerful belief system that focuses its employees on a goal of outstripping its competitors. As founder Jim Casey once said, "Take care of the big things and the small things will follow."

The temperature on Iwo Jima on the morning of February 19, 1945, was somewhere near sixty degrees Fahrenheit. The sky was overcast. There were no seabirds on the island, no songbirds, not even the tiny green lizards that scamper across volcanic islands. After the first bombardments at 2:00 A.M., it seemed that even the five senses had fled. The Japanese enemy was dug into the island like crabs. They hid in tunnels, holes, and caves. "The Japanese fought underground," as one observer described the battle. "The Marines fought aboveground."

For thirty-six days the Marines of the Third, Fourth, and Fifth divisions fought their way across the island step-by-step, using pistols, rifles, grenades, flamethrowers, and bare hands as they battled the twenty-two thousand Japanese dug in on the eight-square-mile island. After three days of heavy fighting and thousands dead on both sides, a patrol of forty

Marines made their way up the side of the island's tallest mountain, Mount Suribachi.

Climbing for over two hours under heavy fire, a bloodied platoon from Echo Company finally reached the top. Once they had placed themselves in defensive positions around the perimeter of the volcanic crater, Marine sergeant Mike Strank ordered the men to raise the American flag on the summit. It was the first American flag raised on Japanese soil. Strank told them to use an oversized flag, so that "every Marine on this cruddy island can see it."

Photographer sergeant Lou Lowery took the first flag-raising picture. When headquarters saw the raised flag, they ordered a second flag raising to take place, and this time AP photographer Joe Rosenthal went along. The famous photograph of February 23, 1945, hit the cover of *Life* magazine and the scene of six Marines raising the American flag became an icon of World War II. (The fact that three of the six men—including Strank—would die in battle soon after the photo was taken was not lost on the millions of Americans waiting back at home.)

The photograph, and the subsequent statue of the flag raising located at Arlington National Cemetery in Virginia, is just one of many icons that can be taken from the United States Marine Corps's over two-hundred-year history. Like many primal organizations the mythos and creed of the Marine Corps affect those who serve far more than their four years of service might account for. Marines feel an esprit de corps unrivaled in the American armed forces. It has been that way for many decades.

"It is the uniformly 'Marine' character of the three United

States Marine Corps divisions that give them their formidable fighting power," says military writer John Keegan. "The mythology of the Marines, expressed in the Marine hymn and the motto *semper fidelis* ("always faithful"), together with a litany of Corps slogans—including, 'A Marine never dies'—has poetic truth. If a recruit chooses to think otherwise, he will be put straight by the long-service NCO of the Corps—gunnery sergeants and sergeant majors—who are tradition's ultimate guardians."

As is true of many primal organizations the icons, rituals, and creed of the Marine Corps run a far deeper course than most other organizations. The creation story of the Corps begins when the Continental Congress passed a resolution on November 10, 1775, asking that "two Battalions of Marines be raised" to serve as landing forces for the fledgling American fleet. Since then, millions of Americans have served in the United States Marine Corps, and their history continues through 1805, when Marines battled the Barbary pirates on the shores of Tripoli for President Thomas Jefferson, onto the fields of Cuba, the Boxer Rebellion, Vietnam, and the wars in Iraq. But the historical creation story doesn't stop there. The legend runs through family histories as well. Many families have a personal history of the Corps, as their fathers, grandfathers, and other family members served in the Marine Corps. Many individuals have a personal creation story that involves the Marine Corps, as indoctrination into the Corps has many aspects that can be life changing, shaping individuals.

"It changed my life," says Chuck Lindberg, the last survivor of the Marines who raised the flag on Mount Suribachi. "It is a brand that is on your soul the rest of your life," adds

Marshall Davidson, a former U.S. Marine Corps captain who now sells corporate real estate in Houston. "And that is not a corny thing. It is a very difficult journey that you take in order to become a Marine."

The Marine Corps creed is about shaping character, as it must be when accepting citizens off the street and turning them into units of trustworthy fighting soldiers. The principles of honor, courage, and commitment are held high in the U.S. Marine Corps. "Marines practice self-discipline to the extreme," declares a recruiting brochure. They find themselves motivated by "the unrelenting determination to achieve a standard of excellence in every endeavor."

Semper fidelis ("always faithful") is not only written in blood in the sands of foreign shores, it has been tattooed on the shoulders of thousands of diehard leathernecks. (Unknown to some, the Marine Corps creed is also shared by England's Devonshire Regiment, the Eleventh Foot.) But the true meaning of *semper fi* is something that cannot be understood by anyone who has not served in the Corps. Mere words to others, they are felt viscerally, tangibly, and unalterably by Marine Corps veterans in a way that others will never truly feel, much less understand.

Rituals in the Marine Corps run long and deep. In the ritual separation from ordinary society, as civilians become Marines—otherwise known as boot camp—recruits ("boots") are shorn of their hair, trade in civilian clothing ("civvies") for ordnance ("O.D.") green, are moved to new living quarters with the rest of their bunk mates ("bunkies"), and quickly learn the language of the Corps. It is a language that might quite literally save their lives.

The "death toll" during Marine Corps training is high. People are weeded out during exercises designed to simulate the stress of battle. The physical and mental fatigue experienced by Marine Corps recruits is legendary. But those who survive have a greater chance of surviving on the real battlefield. "People who can't handle sleep deprivation have no business being on a battlefield," says Davidson. "Because you can't trust them."

The introductory hazing of Marine recruits is another ritual. During six weeks of boot camp young men and women undergo a rigorous program that engages them in physical and weapons training and teaches them an overall dedication to the purposes of the Corps. "They really will destroy whatever allegiance and affiliations existed before," says Davidson. A case in point is kids coming from inner-city gangs: The Marine Corps utterly destroys the old membership. Says Davidson, "I remember enlisted guys saying, 'Hey you're in a new gang now.'"

The final rite of basic training is known as the Crucible, a demanding fifty-four-hour field exercise that requires everything the recruit has learned during thirteen weeks of training. The course is a series of rigorous mental and physical challenges that must be overcome in order to advance through the exercise. After the Crucible, those who succeed are rewarded with a Warrior's Breakfast and can look forward to the graduation ceremony.

The longer a belief system has been in place, the more primal elements including rituals, icons, leaders, and other exist, and the more intermingled they sometimes become. With a two-hundred-plus-year history of tradition and practice, the long-standing traditions of the Corps serve as ritualistic devices that help mold the character and commitment of U.S. Marine Corps members. The eagle, globe, and anchor Marine Corps seal, the United States Marine Drum and Bugle Corps, the Marine Hymn, the enlistment oath, the uniforms, the Marine officer's sword, the silent drill platoon, and Marine Corps headquarters located at Eighth and I streets in Washington, D.C., are all icons that bespeak the loyalty, dedication, and heritage of America's toughest fighting men and women.

What is curious, says Davidson, is that there is no real reason for the Marine Corps to exist. The Army, Navy, and Air Force do every single job of the Marine Corps, making the Corps itself redundant. "But any congressman or senator who would suggest that would be thrown out of office," asserts Davidson.

One would be hard-pressed to find anyone who didn't believe in the military efficiency and ability of the United States Marine Corps. "Marines are admired throughout the American armed forces and beyond," writes John Keegan. "Particularly by the British army and the Royal Marines, who served with the USMC in Korea and the First Gulf War." Only the men obliged to face Marines in battle must regard themselves as nonbelievers when facing the ferocity of the Corps. These pagans, of course, are the enemies the Marines encountered on battlefields in Tripoli, Iwo Jima, and the Persian Gulf. Other nonbelievers in the Marine Corps would be the competing United States armed services, including the Army, Navy, and Air Force.

The sacred words are the marine enlistment oath, the

nomenclature and argot of the Marine Corps and, of course, *semper fi.*

The leaders of the Marine Corps are the chain of command that begins with the commander-in-chief (the president of the United States) and descends through the Marine Corps commandant, generals, and battalion commanders to the experienced noncommissioned officers and drill sergeants who are the heart and spirit of the Corps.

"The thing I thought was best about the organizational structure of the Marine Corps," says Marshall Davidson, "is that they are constantly refining it, constantly trying to make it organizationally *thin*—thin out the bureaucracy. In fact, fat organizational structures are not celebrated. People are fired for having fat organizational structures, because it's worthless. Marine officers lead from the front."

Davidson elaborates. "The Corps lets the leaders on the ground make the decisions. All organizations ought to be doing that. The people on the ground, like the young lieutenant, they know better than somebody at the rear because the guy at the top is not in the field. There has to be a delegation of authority without delegating away responsibility. And that is critical. Marine officers can be fired for *not* making a decision."

It is the essential character of the United States Marine Corps that individuals are transformed from untrained civilians into dedicated fighting men and women who feel an innate bond with fellow Marines and the spirit of the Corps itself. In fact, virtually every aspect of the organization of the Marine Corps is focused on this transformation and continued commitment.

When viewed from the primal perspective, it is easy to outline how the journey from raw recruit into a dedicated member of the Corps occurs. Each piece of the primal code is entrenched. The creation story is woven through the history of the nation and the legacies of families, the hardened creed, the iconic images and sounds, sacred words like *semper fi,* the nation's enemies as nonbelievers, and the experienced, muscled leathernecks who are the first line of Marine Corps leadership. The result is hundreds of thousands of people who feel they belong to the Marine Corps, whether they serve today or served fifty years ago. The manifestation of the primal code is a hard-core fighting organization of strength and courage, both admired and feared by those who encounter it. They wave to one another at stoplights, greet each other in parking lots, and recount their experiences at reunions. Even would-be belongers who spot the Marine Corps decal stuck on a car bumper will raise their hand in salute and shout to the driver, *"Semper fi!"*

"America loves Marines," says Marshall Davidson. "They love them because they fight and die for their country, for their Corps, for their way of life."

In 1983, Stonyfield Farm opened its barn doors with little more than a handful of dairy cows and a recipe for yogurt. Today, Stonyfield Farm sells 5 or 6 million cups of yogurt a week. It is the third largest brand of yogurt sold in the United States, and as the largest natural and organic yogurt producer in the country, Stonyfield Farm finds itself at the front of the organic movement.

In the beginning, there was Sam Kaymen. It was Sam's

farm, Sam's cows, Sam's yogurt recipe. One of the first biodynamic soil experts in America, Sam started the Rural Education Center in the rocky hills of New Hampshire as an effort
to spread the word about organic farming. He and his wife,
Louise, and their kids fed and milked and cared for their tiny
herd of Jersey cows. In the end, that's what Stonyfield Farm
is still about. As corporate farms bulldoze family farms
Stonyfield Farm's bottom-line success with small organic
farmers has demonstrated that going back to organic can
mean big business.

"Our core principle is that we want to prove that it is not
only possible but highly profitable to be environmentally
committed," says Gary Hirshberg, Stonyfield Farm's CEO.
"It *was* a hypothesis; it is now proven. We go to great pains to
demonstrate the cost-benefit ratios, the return on investment
of all of our environmental investments. And I can say hands
down that they pay." The rewards come in the form of customer loyalty, cost savings, revenue generation—any way
you want to measure success, says Hirshberg.

Stonyfield Farm has five core values that are printed on
the back of every business card. That creed includes providing quality certified organic products; offering consumers
health education; being good corporate stewards; offering a
healthful and productive place for coworkers; and delivering
good returns for investors. Stonyfield has other commit-
ments, too. The company promotes public responsibility, and
10 percent of its profit feeds organizations dedicated to pro-
tecting and restoring the planet. They are actively against the
genetically engineered recombinant bovine growth hormone
(rBGH) that is in popular use on many farms today. And

they proactively figure out ways to reduce their corporate environmental impact. Their steadfast credo has earned them the National Award for Sustainability in the category of atmosphere and climate from the President's Council on Sustainable Development and Renew America; the Corporate Environmental Steward Award from the Council on Economic Priorities; and the Climate Wise Achievement Award from the Environmental Protection Agency.

The rituals for Stonyfield Farm surround yogurt manufacturing and organic farming. Part of this happens inside the corporate culture of Stonyfield Farm, which is robust. Yogurt is one of the oldest milk products in existence, with beginnings thousands of years ago in Bulgaria (hence one of the active yogurt cultures is named *L. bulgaricus*). The ritual of bringing in raw milk and transforming it into product is a time-honored rite that Stonyfield tries to keep as close to its original form as possible. Hirshberg remembers a day in 1987, when he and other Stonyfielders took a tour of a food-processing plant to see if there was anything to be learned from these experts. They had only been in business five years at the time and were, by Hirshberg's admission, naive and still learning. They were horrified by what they saw. "We looked at this thing and said, We'll never be like that, we're never going to do it that way," recalls Hirshberg. "We looked at the ways they were managing large batches and we couldn't believe they could manage the correct quality." Today Stonyfield Farm is at least seven times larger than the company they visited back in 1987.

In 2000, according to the U.S. Department of Agriculture, more organic food was being sold in supermarkets than in any other venue. That meant organic was no longer banished to food co-ops and roadside stands; it's big business. "They see organic as the way the market is going," Hirshberg says of the Danone buyout in 2004. And with sales growing organically at 20 percent a year, Stonyfield is Danone's tiny experiment. If Stonyfield can continue to grow and demonstrate the effectiveness of organic farming as well as eating, well, who knows?

The sacred words for Stonyfield use the vernacular of dairy farming and yogurt production. Hirshberg's title, for example, is not CEO but "CE-Yo." There is plenty about Stonyfield Farm that has a folksy whimsy ring to it, and just when it starts to get aggravating (for example, when "Moos" replaces the word "news," as in "Moos from the Farm"), you remember that it's all in healthy fun. No pun intended. "Organic" and "earth friendly" are sacred words central to Stonyfield Farm. So are "wellness", "family farms," "inulin," "probiotics," and *Lactobacillus bulgaricus.*

There are many skeptics—nonbelievers—about the efforts of Stonyfield Farm. An active food-processing industry dominates the way food is managed, handled, and created. Corporate farming is the rule; organic farms are still the exception. Yet Stonyfield Farm is committed to keeping antibiotics, growth hormones, pesticides, and other toxins out of their dairy products. And they follow that commitment from soil to yogurt cup. The logic sounds natural. If there are no pollutants in the soil, then they won't be in the grass that the cows eat, or in the milk the cows produce to create the yogurt that goes into your mouth.

That's all good stuff. But it is an ideal that is tough to hold to. Right now, there is an organic milk shortage. Not enough organic farmers with enough cows, not enough organic farmers with enough grain to feed the organic cows that do exist to help them produce the higher yields. Result? Less organic milk.

The icons for Stonyfield Farm include the Jersey cow-centric logo. Its bucolic Web site with bovines wagging their tails. The taste of Stonyfield Farm can be said to be iconic because, well, it just tastes better. The yogurt cups are shorter and squatter than competitors, giving them a distinct look at shelf. And, of course, Sam Kaymen is also an icon of sorts.

The leaders include founder Sam Kaymen and Gary Hirshberg, the CEO who has been with Stonyfield almost from the beginning. In the end, the real ingredient in their yogurt company is a better way of creating commerce. "Our real mission is to change the way companies like Danone and General Mills do their business," says Hirshberg, who once ran an environmental nonprofit. "They can do more good with one purchase order than I can do in my lifetime."

Production integrity, quality products, and an equal portion of primal code is how Stonyfield Farm finds itself at the front of the organic movement. Now almost completely owned by its parent conglomerate Group Danone (in 2004 Danone gained control of 80 percent of the stock), Stonyfield Farm is the number-one-selling organic food in the country. The dual challenge of creating a market for its product while simultaneously creating organic supply for its product is a two-horned dilemma most companies do not face. Stonyfield Farm has been experiencing 20 percent annual growth for ten years or more. Today there are twenty thousand natural food stores around the country, and most of them carry Stonyfield Farm. Organic products are in over 70 percent of conventional stores, and as consumers continue to pay for organic products, that number will continue to increase. But sales numbers are not the only issue for Stonyfield Farm.

"In order for there to be a healthy planet, family farmers have to be a part of the mix," insists Hirshberg. Even in the face of short supply, Hirshberg is consistent in his vision. "Organic agriculture is our highest objective," he declares. And then, an organic CE-Yo to the end, Hirshberg says, "We're all compost sooner or later. You want to make the most of your short time here."

It is a cold winter's day. The sky is scraped blue. Black squirrels crawl through the branches. Out on the warp, where the sprawl of housing developments and industrial parks meet the edge of rolling Minnesota prairie, rests the headquarters of Aveda Corporation. Best known for its shampoos and skin and body products, Aveda is a manufacturer, wholesaler, and retailer of personal care and lifestyle products that operates in twenty-seven international markets and has over eight thousand salons around the world. In 1997, Aveda was sold to Estée Lauder.

Aveda was started in 1978, when founder Horst Rechelbacher, the son of herbalist parents, stood in his hair salon and smelled the chemical concoctions he and the other stylists were pouring onto clients' heads. He decided that he wanted to be surrounded by products that he could be proud of, that had been made in a way that would not harm his clients or himself. The motivation seems almost selfish, admits Chris Hacker, senior vice president of marketing and design. But the result has been not only dozens of products in a category known for chemical excess, but a company overwhelmingly committed to environmental responsibility. "The primary key from our perspective," says Hacker, "is that we are a mission-driven business that believes environmental responsibility and profitability are not mutually exclusive." "At Aveda" writes Horst Rechelbacher in the company's mission statement, "we strive to set a responsible level of environmental leadership, not just in the world of beauty but around the world."

That creed resonates through everything that is done at Aveda. When the company develops products they search for ingredients that come from organic or biodynamic sources. Environmental responsibility and leadership is included not only in the products, but in the salons and corporate offices as well. Packaging and product catalogs are created with as much postconsumer recycled content as possible. Displays are made from recycled materials. Hacker gives an example. "The carpet in my office in 90 percent postconsumer recycled carpet. The ceiling tile is made from recycled jute, the desk is made from wheat board, not wood. It's that kind of environmental responsibility that really is the key to what Aveda's about."

One of Aveda's most iconic pieces of code are its aromas (not scent, not fragrance—"aroma"). While many hair care and fragrance companies build around single ingredients— they develop a product line that is citrus, another that is woody, the next tropical—Aveda's approach is more complex. They combine aromas to create something that has never been sensed before.

"We are much more interested in a characteristic, complex aroma that is hard to identify," declares Hacker, "but is wonderful." Aveda aromas can contain over fifty different pure essences from fruits, nuts, flowers, and bark. It should come as no surprise, then, that Aveda's ingredients lists includes things most of us have never heard before: Annatto. Petitgrain. Soapwort. Vetiver. Touralmine. Ylang ylang. Cupuacu. Buriti. Japanese knotweed. Babassu. Iceland moss. Oh, and pennywort. "We consider aromas an icon within the context of the company," says Hacker. "We always consider aroma to be a critical part of what people perceive the difference to be in Aveda, from other products of the same use or function."

Peter Matravers, vice president of research and development, goes further. "We utilize aroma beyond pleasant smell," he says. "We have mood-mapping and various aromatherapeutic studies that invoke certain responses such as calming, energizing," he explains. "And we are doing research to find out the mode of action or mechanism of action behind this." For example, while peppermint might be invigorating, it is also an appetite suppressor. (So while it might be great for hair gel, you wouldn't want to spray it around a grocery store or restaurant.) Aveda has coined two terms for that difference: "aroma-active" and "aromatherapeutic."

The Aveda aroma you notice when you walk into a retail store or a salon is their Shampure shampoo product. "It has a denseness and a kind of richness that people recognize immediately," says Hacker. "Usually when people walk into the salon they'll say, 'Ooh, this is amazing!' If they know Aveda, they'll say, 'Oh, this is an Aveda salon.'"

Developing aromatherapy-based products takes an average of eighteen months. There are job-based rituals centered on the corporate philosophy that go into the creation of Aveda products. The main effort is seeking out all the certified organic oils that exist on the planet. Efficacy of the product is key, and in some cases judging the aroma's active role in the shampoo, conditioner, or moisturizer can take up the greatest time portion in the development process.

But it goes deeper than that. Aveda has embarked on a "soil to bottle" program that is steeped in their commitment to bettering their products, their communities, and the planet at large. "When we make a product," says Matravers, "we ask ourselves the following questions. Performance: Is this better than what's out there already? The second question: Is this botanical? Because we certainly don't want an ingredient to be man-made. The third question we ask: Is this innovative? Is it something that will green the earth as we make the product? Another element that we ask ourselves: Is this pleasurable to use or experiential? Using an Aveda product is not just about smelling good; it must evoke a higher level of sensation. And then the last question we ask ourselves: Are we doing something positive for the community? Are we giving new hope? Are we preserving cultural biodiversity?"

This philosophical exploratory during new product exploration is rare in corporate America. It is also time consuming and expensive. And while high-minded sociopolitical ideals make nice corporate philosophy, dealing with local personalities at ground level can be an enervating time suck. "We don't have to do it," shrugs Matravers. Petrochemical substitutes abound. "But these actions make Aveda unique."

Consider the babassu. The babassu nut grows in the

forests of Brazil, where an indigenous people has been harvesting them since time began. Local ranchers wanted to clear the forests where the valued babassu tree grew—for cattle range. The two agricultural communities stood head to head until finally legislation was passed that prohibited cutting down the trees. Local women were allowed to "wild craft"—go into forests and pick up the fallen nuts that are their cash crop and a valuable part of their culture. The babassu nuts are pressed for their precious oils, which are used as foaming agents in Aveda products. The nuts are also consumed by locals as a food product. The nut is high in protein and therefore makes great chicken feed. The husks are turned into charcoal for fuel.

"It's a win-win situation," says Matravers. "They in turn become the stewards of their land, and are able to grow things with great traceability. All our essential oils in aroma right now are all organically grown. So we also contribute to the organic focus and organic movement globally."

Of course, it's on the street where Aveda has made its mark. The seven thousand retail shops and salons spread around the world are loaded with ritual events. At most salons, you're met at the door with a tray of tea, or offered your beverage of choice. The person may introduce you to a scalp massage while consulting with you about your hair. These ritual store experiences not only differentiate Aveda, they are customer enhancing. "The idea of coming into a salon, having a cup of tea, being given a hand massage, sitting down for your consultation, and then going to the shampoo bowl and having a stress-relieving treatment, it just changes your point of view," says marketing chief Hacker.

"We talk about it as, Making your day. Changing the way your day has gone by taking you out of the stress of what you've experienced before."

Helping employees understand Aveda values is a daily task. Horst Rechelbacher's credo hangs in the lobby in Minnesota headquarters and is reiterated in one form or another at the thousands of Aveda salons. There is also extensive training at Aveda institutes around the country. At Experience Aveda sessions, stylists, managers, and other employees receive training on the products. "We put as many people through the process as possible," says Chris Hacker. "There's a class going on somewhere every day of the week." And at twenty-two Aveda institutes around the country young people are trained in the Aveda aesthetic and create a talent pool Aveda can draw from. (Students may work anywhere they like, even for a competitor, after their Aveda training.) It's incredibly important to communicate to employees. After all, if employees don't understand the Aveda essence, how can they communicate it to customers? "We spend a lot more on it than most people would," says Chris Hacker, "because we know it's a point of difference."

At the end of the day Aveda is a retail operation, and even the mundane is imbued with essential oils. Instead of a typical spreadsheet, at the end of the retail day store managers fill out a form titled "The Ritual of Success" with comments and sales figures.

Sacred words in the Aveda lexicon (Aveda itself is a sacred word, and comes from the Sanskrit *a veda* which means "all knowledge") include "soil to bottle," "aroma-active," "aromatherapeutic," "organic certified," "making your day." Of course, trademarked product lines like "Shampure" also fall into Aveda usage, as well as names of the esoteric nuts, fruits, and flowers that Aveda coaxes into essential oils, aromatherapeutic properties, and other purposes like "Jabuticaba," "guava extract," "vetiver oil," "cardomam."

Those who do not believe in the Aveda spirit—pagans—would be manufacturers of cosmetic products that are not organic. Those companies who similarly create vertical aroma themes—for example, drugstore jasmine, strawberry, and citrus lines. And, of course, the ranchers who slash the forests filled with babassu trees. It is a paradox.

"We have this highly fashion-driven business that we're involved in," says Chris Hacker. "Hairdressers wanting to be up to the moment in what they're putting on their clients, because they're driven by the fashion shows." As we're talking, the New York fashion show is happening, and Aveda is doing the hair for twenty-five designers, including Vera Wang and Betsey Johnson. "There's this dichotomy," continues Hacker, "between this earthy-crunchy developing products in a way that is environmentally responsible, and then making sure they're making the coolest products that people can use in a way that's highly fashionable and really cool."

In one of the most competitive categories that exists, Aveda is hugely successful. In 2004, Aveda won the Cooper-Hewitt Corporate Achievement Award for its floor-to-shelf aesthetic and corporate responsibility.

As we walk through the Aveda R&D labs I am reminded how the beauty business is built upon subjective aesthetics that are essentially superficial. Yet, Aveda has created a point of view that is immensely rich in spirit and cash. It might have been so different. I remember sitting in the office of a CEO of another shampoo company. For a frustrating hour she sat fiercely close-lipped as we tried to suggest that her shampoo products could mean more to people than just pretty hair. At the height of her frustration the red-faced CEO stood up and screamed, "It's just dead cuticle, people!" That CEO's misunderstanding of cuticle paralleled her misunderstanding of her product's potential.

Inside the Aveda warehouse barrels, boxes, and plastic containers filled with aromatherapeutic essence are warehoused floor to ceiling. Peter Matravers and I pass an industrial-size two-hundred-gallon tank of babassumidopropyl betaine—and pause. This is the product of the babassu wild harvest women in Brazil. Not only are consumers being offered a better product, but a forest is saved, fewer people move from the arboreal forest to city slums, a way of life is sustained. "Instead of simply satisfying a consumer need, we want to green the earth and excite the human spirit," says Peter Matravers. As we move on, he sighs. "It's what we can do to make things better."

The primal code is all part of a narrative; it is storytelling. When pieces of the story are missing, the story becomes less interesting, people become less interested. When people sense that pieces of primal code are missing, they feel dissatisfied and turn away.

Somewhere there is a parallel statistic: 99 percent of dissatisfied customers don't complain; they just walk away (and don't come back).

*   *   *

I am sitting inside a restaurant next to a group of middle-aged women. The unusual thing about these women is that they are all wearing large, oversized, floppy red hats. It is clear that the hats are not only a ticket to the table, they are an unspoken license for something else. No two hats are exactly alike, but they are all similar in their madcap, saucy, goofy spirit. Finally, I have to ask.

"Why the hats?" They are members of the Red Hat Society, one of the women smiles. Well, naturally.

The Red Hat Society was founded seven years ago by Sue Ellen Cooper of Fullerton, California. The whole thing started when she bought a red fedora at a thrift store as a cheap thrill. She was so pleased, she started buying the iconic red hats for friends as joke gifts. After a while, so many of Sue Ellen's friends had hats, she decided it would be fun if they all went out together wearing them. It would be silly. You know, a girl group.

Inspired by a poem by Jenny Joseph titled "Warning," in which a young woman pledges to don a red hat and a purple dress and celebrate her age, Sue Ellen and her friends threw on their colors and went to tea. Wherever they went they attracted attention. The press followed. In July 2000, they were featured in *Romantic Homes* magazine. Their notoriety spread. Other groups popped up. More media.

"It's a women's play group, pure and simple," says Queen Mother Sue Ellen Cooper. "It's permission to play. It turned into sisterhood, too, because women do bond."

Today there are over 850,000 Red Hat Society members around the world, and over 36,000 chapters. And the numbers keep growing. "We have a new chapter in Thailand," laughs Sue Ellen.

Wherever these women meet, they're there to have a ball. They call it their "disorganization," which adds to the group's atmosphere of fun and frolic, which is, after all, what it's all about. Says Sue Ellen, "The spirit is all-inclusiveness, friendliness, kindheartedness, generally a cheerful spirit." The icons are as easy to spot as the floppy red hats. The *Red Hat Society Lifestyle* magazine, the character Ruby RedHat, even a Red Hat Society membership pin. The queen bee herself also receives icon status.

The lunches, teas, and special gatherings are all ritualized events, even if there is no standard way of doing it. Sue Ellen explains, "Everybody does exactly their own thing. You might decide to go miniature golfing, go to dinner, go away for the weekend, have a big party. We are totally free-form. It's all about sharing and giving each other ideas."

Every Friday, Sue Ellen sends an e-mail from Hatquarters that she calls her "Friday broadcast." The ritual Friday broadcast is actually a tongue-in-cheek Internet newsletter. The broadcast lets everyone know what's going on at other chapters. It is loaded with funny anecdotes and constant reminders of how to spread the word about RHS.

"Helpful hint for the day," Sue Ellen advises in one Friday broadcast. "Wear your official membership pin as often as possible. It's small enough that it won't clash in a serious way with your outfit and it's noticeable enough that other Red Hat Society sisters will see it right away."

Who are the pagans? Women who prefer to grow old

rather than play. Red Hatters refuse to be packed away on a shelf; they are the antithesis of women who grow old before their time. The Red Hatters do not want youth; they are proud of the wisdom that comes with their age. They simply want a place that recognizes that they are resoundingly *alive*. As Sue Ellen Cooper writes in their credo, "The Red Hat Society began as a result of a few women deciding to greet middle age with verve, humor and elan."

"Verve" is definitely one of the Red Hat's sacred words. But there are others. Jenny Joseph's poem "Warning" is given legend status. As is the "Ode To The Red Hat Society." There is a "Reduation" ceremony to initiate new members. And there is the online store, which is called "Imperium" (it is the imperial emporium, therefore the Imperium). Clearly, someone has taken on wordsmithery full-time.

The leaders of the Red Hat Society are not only Sue Ellen Cooper (the exalted queen mother), but also the leaders of the thirty-six thousand other chapters spread around the world. They are known as Queen Mothers (only Sue Ellen can be the Exalted Queen Mother), Queen Bees, and Empress. The grander the title, says Sue Ellen, the better.

These women lead local chapters all over the United States and Canada, and are as far flung as New Zealand, the United Kingdom, and Mexico. They go by the name of Red Hatters, but they are also known as the Luscious Lushes, the Red Hot Mamas, the Razzle Dazzle Divas, even the Slightly Outrageous Ladies in Reds and Purples. As the baby boomers of the sixties grow into their sixties, they discover that the Red Hat Society is a great way to discover that life is still fun. "It's a great way to expand your life instead of seeing it contract," says Sue Ellen. "You meet new people and continue to grow as a person instead of gradually ruling things out."

The success of the Red Hat Society begs the question that lies at the root of everything: How can an organization like a Red Hat Society bubble to the surface and claim over 850,000 members worldwide, while other organizations struggle to find membership? You can argue that not all organizations are founded with the purpose of making life a tea party. Yet, with minimum exposure (as compared with the millions of dollars spent in advertising on some brands) they have created a disorganization that rivals many. Surely there is more to it than exposure, interest, and kismet.

The simple fact is that the Red Hat Society has found the primal code. And with it, they have garnered a group of spirited women bursting toward 1 million. And why not join in the fun? As Sue Ellen Cooper declares, "Come out and play with us!"

4. The Primal Destination

As we have seen, the primal code is a way of building a belief system that attracts communities of people. These communities can surround a product or service. They can surround the ideals of a corporate organism, and help to create a corporate culture. The tools of primal branding can surround a personality, like Shepard Fairey, Martha Stewart, Oprah, Tiger Woods, and others. The assets of the primal code can also be used to help create a civic community that people are attracted to, a community that people feel something about and want to belong to.

Communities like New York City, Napa Valley, and Las Vegas would be less attractive without their icons of the Statue of Liberty, the wineries, and the Strip. Those icons immediately summon positive images of those vibrant communities. But there is much more going on there than anyone might suppose.

Times Square is a small chunk of a big city. Yet Times Square is a focal point visited by millions each year. The mass of gawking humanity spills into the eight-block area from all over the world. England. Germany. Tokyo. Singapore. Russia. And everywhere in between.

Originally named Longacre Square after James Barton Longacre, a U.S. Mint engraver, the area was christened Times Square on April 8, 1904, when the *New York Times* moved its offices to the square created within the parallel avenues of Broadway and Seventh. The area instantly became New York's center for theater and music.

Times Square has not always been as bright and robust as it is today, however. The period of elegance began during the turn of the last century and continued through the jazz years and World War II. The zenith of those heady days was on VJ Day in 1945, when Times Square hosted one of its largest gatherings ever. Over 200,000 people gathered in the square to celebrate the victory over Japan, a day immortalized when a Navy sailor grabbed a woman and kissed her as a hundred flashbulbs popped, including those of photographer Alfred Eisenstadt.

In the 1950s, however, the square became a parody of itself. The flashy Broadway theaters became bookended with porno theaters, souvenir stands, drunks, pimps, and hagglers. Some of the most common visitors to the square were not tourists in cargo pants and flip-flops, but hard-core heroin addicts. The low-down urban vibe was picked up by musicians, and writers like Allen Ginsberg and Jack Kerouac who sat in the square and felt the beat, the throb. In fact, the Beat Generation was born in Times Square, in the bars and cafeterias along West Forty-second Street, before it drove out onto the West Side Highway and headed for California. For the next twenty years Times Square was a no-man's land. In the 1990s, Mayor Rudolph Giuliani decided that enough was enough. Flanked by concerned citizen groups and reinforced with funding from business leaders and Walt Disney Corporation, Giuliani closed the strip clubs and porn shops and supported a renovation project that continues to this day.

"Times Square had gone from world famous center of entertainment, a commercial hub, to a place that became shorthand for the worst of the city's negligence and degradation," says Gretchen Dykstra, who was founding president of the Times Square Business Improvement District (BID), the group mandated with the task of turning Times Square around. "It stood for something terrible."

The story of the improvement of Times Square has its own primal roots. Headed by a board that included Arthur Sulzberger (publisher of the *New York Times*), Shubert Organization chairman Gerry Schoenfeld, Tom Reese of Marriott Corporation, the League of American Theaters, the 42nd Street Development Project, as well as other businesses and developers, the BID's mission was to make Times Square clean, safe, and friendly. It was a daunting task. Other politicians, business groups, and concerned citizens had already tried to clean up the square, and failed. "There was an extraordinary level of cynicism of the chances of ever cleaning up Times Square," admits Dykstra. "The skepticism was deep and not unjustified." In 1992, before the square was cleaned, the area was famous for small crimes like pickpocketing, sexual harassment, and a generally sullen vibe. One hotel was threatened with losing their airline housing contract because a stewardess had been stabbed. Three office towers were vacant and bankrupt. In one of her first meetings Dykstra remembers that the owner of the New Year's Eve Ball Drop, also under the pressure of bankruptcy, was threatening to sell the ball to the highest bidder. "It easily could have been dropping an aspirin tablet," quips Dykstra. An even bigger threat was that the famous New Year's Eve ball drop was also losing market share on television.

The BID decided to focus on the Democratic Party's national convention arriving that summer. Working collaboratively, the BID pooled the different constituencies of hotel owners, businesses, and theaters. "The notion of building a sense of community started with helping the board understand that if they worked together, all boats would rise," adds Dykstra. "Neighborhoods that work together are neighborhoods that work." By April 1992, they had outfitted the Times Square sanitation crews with bright red uniforms. They put fifty trained security officers on streets around the square (the officers cannot make arrests but assist New York City Police Department officers). They placed oversized steamer trunks in the square as tourist booths and staffed them to help tourists. When the Democratic convention rolled into town, the press corps was surprised to discover a refreshed Times Square. They were handed scripts with good things to say about the square. They were able to watch *Broadway on Broadway,* the first collaboration between the Broadway theaters and their neighbors.

"The first blush of success came when we began to have a distinct strategy between patrolling the streets, cleaning the streets, working with the homeless, establishing relationships with city agencies, and connecting the hard services," says Dykstra. "The event we chose to do that with was *Broadway on Broadway.*" The networks ran stories about the new Times Square and, over time, Times Square became the place to be again. Theaters were renovated and refurbished, new buildings were constructed, and the neon lights in Times Square grew brighter than ever before. (Times Square is zoned so that you can't build a building without signage.)

Today, over 23 million people visit Times Square each year. That's more than any other spot on the planet except Walt Disney World. The ongoing mission—or creed—is about keeping Times Square a clean, well-lighted place, buzzing with positive energy. With the possible exception of voting and the Fourth of July, the annual ritual of dropping the ball in Times Square is the biggest national event of the year (the ritual drop is owned and trademarked by Countdown Entertainment). For many Americans, the new year begins in Times Square as New Year's Eve is broadcast live on NBC, MTV, BET, and by satellite.

Other rituals that draw people to the square are orchestrated and partnered and managed by the Times Square Alliance and other groups (no single group could be responsible for all the events that go on in Times Square). Teenagers know that Times Square is MTV headquarters (an icon in its own right), and the sidewalk in front of MTV's studios is usually packed with teenagers from Connecticut, Long Island, New Jersey, and Ohio, trying to catch a glimpse of their favorite stars through the second-story studio glass of *Total Request Live* (known in teenspeak as *TRL*). There's A Taste Of Times Square on Restaurant Row, Summer Solstice (a counterpart to New Year's Eve), *Broadway on Broadway,* a

Kissathon to commemorate VJ Day 1945, and dozens of other events. There's probably not a day on the calendar when something isn't happening in Times Square.

"Times Square is in the news practically every day," says one spokesman.

Another simple ritual is people watching. The flow of intersecting human rivers along Broadway and Seventh Avenue and down West Forty-second Street is as expressive and timeless and vast as watching the surf on Malibu Beach. Going to the theater is a ritual. So is waiting in line for your discounted theater ticket at TKTS. Standing looking up at the headbanging neon lights and raving posters is a ritual. Going to see ABC's *Good Morning America* taped live weekday mornings is a ritual. Going to the opening night of a Broadway show is a ritual. Going up to see the *David Letterman Show* after walking the square is a ritual. Stopping in at Colony Records and Rudy's Guitars and the deli inside the Edison Hotel are all rituals. The Times Square Alliance and other organizations constantly come up with more activities to draw more people into the area.

Times Square cannot be walked through. It must be assaulted. During the day, visitors brace themselves against the two hundred thousand people who arrive simply to work in the news and entertainment towers headquartered in the area. By night, there are the limousines and flashy theatergoers. At all times, the swarms of humanity mill under the lights, heads down or heads up, some energized by the urban fair people watching, some intimidated by the shining powers of commercialism glaring down at them. The icons of Times Square include the visual frenzy of semiclad models and illuminated liquor bottles and the nonstop rush of videotronic walls splashing the human cornea with multicolored eye candy. The images are reflected, deflected, and absorbed, the result evident on the smitten faces of tourists and passersby. Recent visitors to Times Square have been greeted with the Naked Cowboy, a guitar-wielding flaxenhaired man clad only in underwear briefs who serenades on the traffic island on West Forty-fifth Street.

Times Square pagans are the skin bars that have relocated to Eighth Avenue. The Off-off Broadway theaters that exist farther downtown. There are also resident New Yorkers, who object to what they call the "Disneyfication" of Times Square. Other pagans are competing destination choices like Rome, Hong Kong, Tokyo, Paris, London, Dubai, and Las Vegas.

It took a community of businessmen and other citizens to plug in the support and services to create the Times Square that is enjoyed today. They believed in their purpose and put together the financial and strategic resources to push past naysayers and create success where others had failed. "I think the person who deserves the greatest credit for understanding that quality of life would make a huge difference was Arthur [Sulzberger]," says Gretchen Dykstra. Times Square has grown out of its homeless addict days to become the second most popular destination in the world. Nothing beats the steady banging of neon light. The growl of mustard-colored taxicabs as they prowl the streets. The surge of shoulder-to-shoulder humanity muscling their way uptown, downtown, crosstown. Tokyo and London try, but they have nothing like it. Paris? Rome? Never mind. Times Square is distinctly American, brilliantly overstated with its arrogant commercialism and brash 24/7/365 hustle. "The spirit of the old Times Square is what defines the new Times Square," says Gretchen Dykstra. "What makes it great is the number of people walking under those fabulous lights, and that's still the case."

New York City has other places, other attractions. Over a million people gathered in Central Park to witness Christo's saffron-colored "The Gates." But nothing can match the spectacle of Times Square.

Currently at 23 million a year, visitorship has surged since 1990. And despite a lull after 9/11, the crowds in Times Square are definitely back. But in a city where numbers seem to matter so much, it's not the numbers at all that matter in Times Square. As another generation once declared, it's the beat.

Irvington, Virginia, is a two-hundred-year-old village where the Rappahannock River meets Chesapeake Bay. A three-hour drive from Washington, D.C., and an hour from the Virginia state capital in Richmond, Irvington lazed for years beneath sleepy pin oaks as a remote farm and shore community.

Originally known as Carter's Creek Wharf, Irvington seems the perfect spot for busy professionals to head to for romantic getaways and holiday weekends. At least, that was the way Bill Westbrook saw it when he purchased The Hope and Glory Inn eleven years ago for $150,000. Originally a boarding school for girls, The Hope and Glory was a two-story Victorian manse with potential.

"It was a disaster of course," says Westbrook. "The building needed to be totally renovated. And I really didn't want it to be a B&B; I wanted it to be a hotel. I always hated the sense of a bed and breakfast, that doily mentality. If you put your feet up, you were putting them up on the owner's table. You were reading the owner's old books, sleeping in the owner's sheets. I hated that. What I really wanted was a hotel." The question was, of course, What kind of hotel? And what would he call it? Westbrook was sitting across the street drinking a beer one steamy August afternoon. He listened to the sounds of workers demolishing the rooms inside his new property. The bells on the nearby Baptist church started ringing, as they ring every afternoon. "Suddenly, I was thinking that what it came down to for all of us was hope and glory," says Westbrook. "And I decided *that* was the name of the inn."

The Hope and Glory needed more than the promise of a good night's sleep, however. An hour's drive and more from the nearest urban areas, it needed a reason for being. Westbrook quickly found a solution. "I wanted to be known as a romantic destination," he says. "I would overcommit to romance and use PR to project that. The secret to me was to overcommit. To drape it in the mysterious." The gardens at The Hope and Glory are overgrown, with lots of vines and honeysuckle and an English cottage garden. One garden is the white garden, where all the flowers bloom in moonlight. In fact, with a description on the Web site that reads "old-fashioned single hollyhocks mix with antique and David Austen roses, artemesias, gooseneck loosestrife, and cottage pinks," it sounds as quaint as an English tea cozy. The hotel is filled with shabby chic furniture and eclectic folk art pieces. An outdoor shower was constructed that, says West-brook, "is the size of some people's kitchens." Everything that went into The Hope and Glory was testimony to West-brook's overcommitment to that promise of romance.

"If you couldn't fall in love at The Hope and Glory Inn," he laughs, "you just were not going to fall in love." The com-mitment paid off. Right away, The Hope and Glory Inn was featured in eight color pages of *Coastal Living* magazine. It was named one of the "101 Best Hotels In the World" by Tatler-Cunard Travel Guide. It was included as one of the "30 Great Inns in the U.S." by *Travel & Leisure* magazine, and got a spot as one of the "Top Ten Most Romantic Inns" by American Historic Inns. But even with all that initial suc-cess, big trouble formed on the horizon. "We got an awful lot of traffic," says Westbrook. "People who came one time. But we had no repeat business, and I was losing money fast," he admits. "What it came down to was that I could either sell The Hope and Glory and suffer the loss. Or I could invest everything I had, roll the dice, and 'brand' the town. I decide to invest in Irvington."

Westbrook bought a row of shops and started renovating. Soon, his Trick Dog Café was serving martinis and grilled snapper to former Secret Service agents from the nation's capital, retired investment bankers from New York City, overage advertising folk, and others who came to chill out in the remote bayside town. Westbrook knew he had a great communications program in place. He knew he had a great product. In primal terms, he had formed the creed for his hotel. (Romance.) He had successfully communicated it to the public, and his iconic hotel front with its picket fences and romantic feeling was square on target. So what was missing?

A realization hit him like a bedpost in the middle of the night. "I asked the manager, What do people say when they call up?" he says. "And they all asked the same thing: What is there to eat, and what is there to do?

"It was all part of a three-legged stool: 'Where are we going to stay? What are we going to see? And what are we going to do?' Why didn't I see that? The town didn't offer enough, *stay/see/eat/do* had to be imbedded in the town." The rituals that visitors expected from a 'romantic setting' were missing. The romantic dinner at a fine restaurant, the hand-holding while shopping, the picturesque romantic strolls. Westbrook set out to overcome those obstacles.

"First, I hired a hospitality partner from one of the major hotel groups. Then, I built a restaurant, a bar, and a block of shops." Each of the new facilities needed to be encoded with its sense of specialness. "The restaurant needed to be unexpected," says Westbrook. "Something you didn't see coming when you came into this little water town."

Irvington figured high in terms of education and income in a survey of Northern Neck area towns, so Westbrook capitalized on the potential. "I decided I would build a picket fence around everything that stood still long enough to put a fence around it," he says. "I invested in false-front architecture." He also built a dental office for his brother, Robert. Because doctors don't really advertise, Westbrook told the architects that they needed to do something with the office. Instead of columns in front, there are ten-foot toothbrushes.

"My brother moved into this small town with no patients.

In each of the last three years he has had the best years of *his entire career,"* asserts Westbrook. "If you asked him, How did you do that? He would answer, It's the building."

"I've come to understand that the brand is the ad," says Westbrook. "I don't do any advertising. I try to overcommit to an idea. In my brother's case I overcommitted to the building. For Trick Dog Café, I overcommitted to the New York City–style restaurant." He brought in a big-city chef. He put martinis on the drink menu. He introduced dishes priced at $18 and $24, which raised eyebrows for locals used to the local $5.99 chicken platter. Within the first year the restaurant and shops opened, The Hope and Glory Inn went into the black.

"Irvington always had water; it had always been a nice, interesting place. What I've tried to do is create interest for new people. This has not always been popular with residents who did not want the town to change. So I have tried to do it responsibly, and within good taste. Even my most ardent critics have to admit that it was careful and that it was with the town's best interest in mind."

Westbrook is currently working on a winery right in the center of town, thereby preserving the agricultural integrity of Irvington. Have Westbrook's efforts been successful? "The businesses are successful on their own," says Westbrook. "It's sort of a vertically integrated business-restaurant, the inn, and now the winery. Visitors go from one to the next, then the next, and hopefully go home happy."

What indicators suggest that Irvington is a brand? "Property values are up 2 percent a month over the last thirty-six months," says Westbrook. "That's 24 percent a year. Nobody I know has made money like that in the stock market. That alone would tell you that Irvington, as a brand promise, is getting through to people." Westbrook, who had spent his career as a successful advertising executive, has learned some things he didn't learn in thirty years on the job. "There's nothing like standing next to your own cash register. If I had known over the last thirty years what I know now, my recommendations would have been more thoughtful and, frankly, less self-interested. My own business over the last ten years has taught me more about being a marketing guy than anything else in my life. It's the richest part of my life."

What is Irvington's creed? Westbrook puts it into his own words. "Irvington is the best of what small towns are. I think Irvington has kind of emerged as the capital of the Northern Neck. It is by far the most interesting and unique, and it is contemporary in its way. It has a real diverse group of folks, many, many of them have led big lives outside of here. And then there are the people who were born here and have lived here all their lives."

There are two groups of people living in Irvington, the "from here's" and the "come here's." "I am definitely a 'come here,'" laughs Westbrook. "People still talk over the back of pickup trucks. Yet you can have a latte. People still get up at three o'clock in the morning and are down in Carter's Creek catching oysters and crabs. And then, on their way back out of the creek, they could pass a $2 million yacht. I don't want a yuppie village. I want to be around people who work with their hands, people who are educated, yet have the wisdom of experience that often comes with not being sophisticated."

The town itself has become an icon of the quintessential small Virginia town. Sunlight plays over flowers planted along the street. The twin tootbrushes that mark the entry to Dr. Robert Westbrook's dentist office lean into the sun. White picket fences are everywhere, testimony to Westbrook's small town ideal. And in a clever twist to the ubiquitous tourist T-shirt, pedestrians strolling Irvington village sidewalks are greeted with spontaneous messages mounted on freestanding metal poles, much like you would find walking through an arboretum. The placards quip things like, "Questions are more important than answers." And, "A fanatic is one who won't change his mind and won't change the subject." Or, "When the gods wish to punish us, they answer our prayers." And, finally, a single word: "Listen."

"There's a spirit in Irvington now that may have existed one hundred years ago, but has not existed since, until relatively recently," says Westbrook. "There was only one concert a year in Irvington. Now we have a whole season of concerts. There's a farmer's market, a lighted Christmas parade. There are five hundred boats down in Carter's Creek to watch the fireworks display on the Fourth of July—you can walk from boat deck to boat deck, it's so crowded. Now we have the Grape Stomp every year, which draws a thousand people."

Not bad for a town of only four hundred people.

"A town is an experiential brand," says Westbrook. "Irvington as a town *is* the ad. It either keeps its promise or it doesn't. If it doesn't live up to its promise, people say, It's a broken value equation and I'm not coming back."

When Westbrook opened a calendar page at the inn when he first started, he couldn't think of anything to write. Today, the calendar's full. "One hundred years ago there was an opera season, there were businesses in town," says Westbrook. "Ten years ago, there were probably two businesses in town. Now there are businesses everywhere." Some of the nonbelievers live in Irvington itself. For over a year Westbrook was attacked in the weekly newspaper's letters to the editor for creating a town that some critics labeled "Billville."

"The harshest critics tended to be people who resisted change and never wanted things to be different," he says. "And you know what, that's something that I could understand. But I did want things to change.

"Most of the critics were people who were already retired, and I wanted to make a living here. I needed to find a way to make good change with integrity, and hopefully win the critics over. To some extent that's happened, but the critics almost wore me out. And then some lifelong resident would come along and pull me aside, someone who had lived here their whole life, and say, 'Bill, you've done a good thing. Just keep going.'" Westbrook chuckles. "I'm still going."

North of the McCullough mountain range, west of Gypsum Wash and not far from Dog Bone Lake, lays a town that for years was a simple Union Pacific railroad stop on the way to the California coast. Located in desert scrub, summer temperatures that leveled out above one hundred degrees Fahrenheit during the summer kept most people away.

In 1931, however, two things happened that changed this town's luck forever. The first was that the largest dam construction project in the world started right out its backdoor. The second was that the state of Nevada legalized gambling. Faster than you can say "jackpot," hundreds and thousands of thirsty Hoover Dam construction workers were pouring into the Las Vegas strip.

Things calmed briefly when the dam finished construction in 1937. But then the Japanese bombed Pearl Harbor and there were soldiers training their guns on the nearby Nellis Gunnery Range. Military personnel on leave ventured to Las Vegas from the training camps in southern California. After the war, big hotels like the El Rancho, the Flamingo, and the Mint started coming in, and suddenly Las Vegas was the most exciting city in the world.

"There's something going on here all the time," says Rossi Ralenkotter, president and CEO of the Las Vegas Convention and Visitors Authority. "It's like New Year's Eve every night." History aside, Las Vegas's true creation story seems to lie around the Rat Pack, Elvis, and historic bouts of gambling, drinking, dining, and the legendary showgirls. "We've always been an adult destination," says Ralenkotter. "We're family friendly, but our messages are directed at the adult marketplace, whether it's on the leisure side or on the business convention side."

Las Vegas means a lot of things to a lot of people. Gamblers, honeymooners, conventioneers, desperadoes, and couples from Des Moines who just want to have fun—over 37 million in all—visit Las Vegas each year. When they arrive, they are greeted by the dazzle of hotels, convention facilities, dining, shopping, spas, golf. "Everything you would want to have in a destination, we have it," says Ralenkotter. "And it's really cutting-edge." Las Vegas means escape, excitement, sexy, fun, and adventure. But extensive research has shown that the real Las Vegas creed is "adult freedom." Their television advertising campaign "Las Vegas Stories" highlights the sometimes real, sometimes alluded to, sometimes embarrassing visitor stories. The tag line, "What happens here, stays here," sums up the city's adult theme.

Las Vegas has always been a city of excess. So it's no wonder that the icons of other lands have been re-created on the desert floor, including Venetian towers, the Eiffel Tower, the Egyptian pyramids. The shark reef attraction at Mandalay Bay holds over 1.5 million gallons of seawater and one hundred animal species.

Not all the Vegas icons have been imported. There are home-bred icons like the tens of thousands of slot machines, roulette wheels, and blackjack tables. And flesh-and-blood icons like Wayne Newton, Siegfried & Roy, showgirls, and Elvis impersonators. Architectural icons include the neon lights that made the Vegas Strip famous, hotels like Caesar's Palace, the Mirage, the Flamingo, Harrah's, and the Golden Nugget. And the gracious newcomers like the Bellagio, the MGM Grand, the Tuscany Suites, Paris Las Vegas, and more.

The most famous Vegas ritual, of course, is gambling. There's pai gow poker, keno, blackjack, Caribbean stud poker, let it ride, craps, roulette, slots, baccarat, bingo, the racetracks, and sports betting on football, basketball, racing, hockey, and more. But today's Las Vegas entrepreneurs realize that gambling is not the only source of entertainment (there was nothing for the wives to do when they grew tired of hanging out at the tables). Today there's shopping at Gucci, Guess, and Christian Dior, caviar facials at the spa, plus golfing. In 1973 there were twelve golf courses; today there are sixty. Wolfgang Puck, Bobby Flay, Emeril Lagasse, Mark Miller, Jean-Georges Vongerichten, and other famous chefs have brought gourmet dining to the gambling strip formerly only famous for gobbling at all-night buffets.

It wouldn't be Viva Las Vegas! without the shows. Today's lineup is just as fabulous as Frank Sinatra, Sammy Davis, Jr., and Ray Charles. In fact, the roster is even more robust. After taking your pick of Wayne Newton, Celine Dion, or Elton John, you can go see Cirque du Soleil, Blue Man Group, Penn & Teller, and dozens of other magicians, comedians, impressionists, and dancers, plus all the different sports venues, from championship boxing to arena football. This is all part of Las Vegas's evolution from regional destination to international star. "We're the most famous national and international resort and convention destination in the world," confirms Ralenkotter. When a professor from Katmandu in Nepal visited the United States recently, he told me, "I knew about Washington, D.C., and I knew about Las Vegas."

When it comes to nonbelievers, towns trying to draw visitors away from Vegas are the first line. Today there are many convention options to choose from. "The travel and convention industry is a highly competitive industry," says Ralenkotter. "Communities have recognized the value of tourism, the jobs that tourism creates, the revenue that tourism brings in." And Las Vegas is no longer the only place to gamble. Today, every major metropolitan area in the country is within a four-hour drive of a gaming location.

In terms of sacred words, the gamblers' argot qualifies, and also terms like "the Strip," "Vegas," "comped rooms," "one-armed bandit," "What happens here stays here," "show-girls," and others.

The leaders of Las Vegas include the corporations and entrepreneurs who continue to make the city alive and vibrant. Ralenkotter nails the key ingredient for all brands: Reinvention. "The destination keeps reinventing itself," he says.

At night, the glow of dazzling lights on the Las Vegas strip can be seen fifty miles away. From the air, it glitters like a sparkling jewel. Las Vegas is one of the most popular destinations in the world, in part because it shines with primal code. One frequent visitor describes Las Vegas best. "When you're flying in at night and you see the lights down there, you get this tingle," he says. "You really get the feeling that by being in this place your life could change. It's a dream city."

Napa Valley got its independence the year of the American bicentennial, 1976. During a wine-tasting event held in Paris that year, surprised French oenophiles declared two Napa Valley wines as the top of their class. The top red at the French competition was a Stag's Leap Wine Cellars '72. The award-winning chardonnay was a Chateau Montelena '73. Two other Californians also joined the ranks: a white Spring Mountain '73 and Chalone '74 from Monterey County. This stomping of such revered names as Mouton Rothschild, Hout-Brion, and Mersault-Charmes was inconceivable. The United States winners were not well known, for in 1976 even the most knowledgeable Americans alleged that "Gallo wine was fine." What's more, the award-winning wines were hardly even available in California (by the way, in 1976 the award-winning bottle of Stag's Leap sold for six dollars).

The Napa Valley was first settled in 1836 when George de la Concepcion Yount was awarded a Spanish land grant of nine thousand acres. Yount had been a celebrated mountain man, trapping shoulder to shoulder with men like Kit Carson, Jim Bridger, and Jedediah Smith. After blazing a trail that connected Santa Fe to Los Angeles known as the "Old Spanish Trail," Yount settled on his Napa Valley land to raise fruit, vegetables, and livestock. He also built a lumber mill and a gristmill. There is no record of grapes.

Decades later, the towns of Napa, Yountville, Oakville, Rutherford, St. Helena, and Calistoga sprang up. Italian immigrants moved into the valley and planted grape vines. Today, with 280 wineries, Napa Valley has the largest concentration of wineries on the planet. The credo of Napa Valley is to produce the finest wines in the world. The valley hosts rich volcanic soil and a nearly perfect combination of warm and cool temperatures for growing grapes. In fact, in a rare act, the wineries have legislated themselves into an agricultural preserve. The valley's theme—"To a wine grape, it's Eden"—places more emphasis on the grape than the wine, but the area is certainly Eden for wine lovers as well.

Icons for the region include the Napa hills, swollen with rows of grape vines. Some of the wineries themselves, like Opus One, Silverado, and Mondavi, have become icons in their own right. The wine bottles, shaped differently for chardonnay than for cabernet sauvignon, are also iconic. So are the wine barrels and tasting rooms. The labels, of course, are also icons for particular wines, from the stately woodcuts and etchings on labels for Groth, Cakebread Cellars, and Buehler Vineyards, to the more elaborate and colorful illustrations for Sawyer Cellars, Truchard Vineyards, and the Ardente Winery.

Only an hour's drive from San Francisco, Napa area wineries were originally a local and regional point of interest. Today, weekend traffic jams on Highway 29 are a frustrating part of the ritual visit to wine country. Figures vary, but most head counts indicate 3 to 4 million people visit Napa Valley each year from all over the world. While many of the wines are complex, the rituals for visiting Napa Valley are fairly straightforward. Visitors can choose from Stag's Leap just outside of the town of Napa to Chateau Montelena at the northern end of the valley—home of that 1976 award-winning chardonnay. Once on site, the tasting of the wine is a time-honored European ritual cherished by vintners. The combination of taste and smell delights the sophisticated connoisseur, and Napa Valley wines offer much to enjoy. (Anyone who saw the movie *Sideways* is probably familiar with those rituals.)

The deepest ritual, of course, is the ancient rite of harvest, an event almost as old as man. While Napa's celebrations are more sedate than the fertility rites that accompanied primeval harvests, they are no less important. "The harvest is everything," says Opus One CEO David Pearson. "The essential moment in wine-making is the decision as to when and what day and what time you pick the grapes." These days, that moment is a combination of technology and art. The modernization of grape-growing agriculture also includes some firm steps backward. "The leading edge of leading practices," says Pearson, "is rediscovering the most ancient and the oldest practices. For example, we harvest everything by hand. We do as much work in the vineyard by hand as possible."

Where there is wine, there is food. The tables of Napa Valley are no less famous than its wines. People make reservations two months in advance to celebrated restaurants like The French Laundry just to be able to enjoy their sauteed moulard duck foie gras with oven-roasted brooks cherries, black pepper brioche and cherry gastrique. There are other restaurants, like Miramonte, Julia's Kitchen (named after Julia Child), Mustards Grill, Terra, Bistro Don Giovanni, and other spots where the chefs fuse local produce with remarkable recipes and, of course, remarkable local wines. And there's even more for visitors to do. Hot-air balloons, the Calistoga hot springs, the Napa Valley Wine Train, the museum, the racetrack, mineral waters, marathons, the mustard festival, and photography contests.

When it comes to pagans, it's not just about people who don't care for great wine. It's about other regions following Napa Valley's example. Nearby California regions like Sonoma County, San Luis Obispo, and the coastal regions also offer new wines and rival destinations. Today, every state in the union boasts a wine industry, even Alaska (try the Salmonberry). Other pagans, naturally, include people who would rather taste free brewery tour samples of Budweiser or Leinenkugel from Dixie cups.

The way that vintners talk about wine is more poetry than prose. Read this excerpt on the sauvignon blanc grape: "hints of straw, hay, grass, meadow, smoke, green tea, green herbs, and gunflint charge around in your mouth with wonderful intensity." This is not boilerplate; these are sacred words.

Names like "Opus One," "Stag's Leap Cask 23," and "Joseph Phelps Insignia" also have been canonized by wine connoisseurs. Their names resonate with meaning. Even wines from lower stratospheres like PlumpJack, Groth, Frog's Leap, and Cakebread Cellars are richly meaningful.

The leaders of Napa Valley are the vintners creating the legendary wines, the chefs like Chef Thomas Keller of French Laundry who keep the tables warm, and the civic leaders who keep the community vibrant and alive. The story of Napa Valley is lush with history, incredible food, and rich wines. And it is also an award-winning blend of the primal code.

At 25° 18' N, 55° 18' E, the water is a color blue usually reserved for precious jewels. Below the water are coral reefs perfect for diving and snorkeling. The warm sand is the color of snow. Overhead, thousands of date palms sway in a breeze coming off the Arabian sea. The day is perfect, the setting pristine. It is a day in paradise.

This is the Palm Jumeirah, a resort on the Arabian peninsula that is the dream of His Highness Sheikh Mohammed bin Rashid Al Maktoum. Envision 2,400 beachside apartments and 50 luxury hotels, as well as theme parks, restaurants, sports facilities, health spas, shopping areas, and movie theaters.

One problem. If you want to book a reservation at the Palm immediately, no luck. The Palm is a man-made island (in the shape of a date palm tree, naturally) that won't be ready until the summer of 2006. Until then, sand, geotextile filter, small rocks, and larger stones—over 7 million metric tons of rock quarried from all over the United Arab Emirates—are being layered on top of one another to create the breakwater and above-sea-level terra firma.

Satellite cameras observe the progress of over five hundred laborers working around-the-clock to create this vacation paradise. Did you miss that? The Palm is so large, it can be seen from outer space. (Potential investors or homeowners are invited to observe progress on the Internet.) And there's not just one Palm. Three Palm resort areas are being built by Nakheel, the Dubai premier real estate development firm. The first is the Palm Jumeirah. Its sister development, the Palm Jebel Ali, is twenty-five kilometers away, with a completion date of 2008, and Palm Deira won't be ready until 2010. (A seven-thousand-square-foot villa with seven bedrooms and its own private beach runs for a little over $2 million.)

The creation story for this out-of-this-world project is also out of this world. According to rumor, a few years ago the regent of Dubai realized that his oil reserves were running low. In fact, his experts informed him, his oil wells were going to run dry within his lifetime. Weighing the possible alternatives, his highness decided to transform Dubai from a dubious oil principality into what the promotion materials call "one of the world's premiere travel destinations."

The creed is clearly stated in the promotional materials for the Palm, which is to create the "8th wonder of the world." You can forgive the hyperbole when you realize that hyperbole is exactly what is right about the Nakheel project. After all, laying down 7 million metric tons of rock is nothing short of creating a world wonder. (Quick math calculates that the Great Pyramid of Giza is a mere 5.2 million tons.) And what is more hyperbolic than building a palm tree in the middle of the sea?

The island's date palm tree shape, which promotional materials refer to as "the bride of the desert," is utterly iconic. So is the shape of another Nakheel development in the works. The World, shaped in a Mercator map version of planet Earth, is replete with eight continents and both poles.

And remember Irvington, Virginia. The town was stagnating without its sense of small town-ness—the white picket fences and flowered gardens, the Fourth of July celebrations. What is right about the Palm Jumeirah is exactly its sensibility of an "ultimate" and "extraordinary" location. All the icons of a relaxed ultimate experience are in place: the pools, the deep water diving, the luxury appointments, spas, workout rooms, upscale shopping, and other details that signal an extraordinary experience.

With one of the most fantastic undertakings in the world, it is easy to find doubters. The obvious pagans for this larger-than-life undertaking include all the less likely destinations on the planet.

His Highness Sheikh Mohammed bin Rashid Al Maktoum is the undisputed man with the vision behind these developments. But there are other leaders at the over forty consulting firms involved in the project. The daily tasks of dredging and building architectural structures involves myriad managers, supervising architects, engineers, and technicians, all necessary leaders for completion of the task.

It is for the sands of time to decide if the Palm and its sister projects will become success stories. But they seem to be on the right track.

Some of the same things that attract people to come visit also entice them to stay. Luxury apartments in the Times Square area are selling at luxury prices. Housing prices in Irvington, Virginia, are rising at double-digit percentage points. There is no deeper sense of place and community than the town or neighborhood in which you live. Once a belief system is developed around a geographic community, the same thing happens that happens when you create a NikeTown—people are drawn to it. They *believe* it is a better place to live and raise their families and prefer to live there rather than anywhere else.

By placing the pieces of primal code in your community you can make a desirable community even more desirable. You can make an area that does not seem to have much going for it—like Times Square or desert real estate—into an attractive nexus. (If you can turn around a blighted area filled with hookers and drug addicts into a boom town, anything seems possible.)

You can also attract commerce, which Times Square proves with its continued influx of entertainment and financial companies. And Las Vegas entrepreneurs keep adding new hotels, restaurants, golf courses, and other new enterprises. "More people want to start businesses," says Bill Westbrook in Irvington, Virginia, "but there's just not enough land." Add the primal code into a healthy mix of jobs, education, social services, and good plumbing and your town might find itself on the next list of America's most livable cities.

5. The Primal Personality

"**I**'m Nobody!" screamed Emily Dickinson in her famous poem. Her anguished cry from 150 years ago still registers as we walk down Fifth Avenue or through The Mall of America and find ourselves surrounded by millions of nobodies. Most of us lead lives of quiet anonymity. We gape from a distance as athletes like Tiger Woods and teens like Lindsay Lohan and Ashley Simpson rise to glory. We don't usually think of television and movie stars and media celebrities as brands, but they are. They seemingly rise at random, walk the red carpet, cover the pages of *People* magazine, sit on the couch next to David Letterman and across the table from Charlie Rose. We leer as they appear in television commercials and in print advertising. Some stand the test of time. Others, having enjoyed their fifteen minutes of fame, come back and join the rest of us in the bleacher seats.

But how do they rise to our attention in the first place? Listen to the radio. You'll often hear a new band introduced, and the DJ will tell how the members grew up together in Manhattan Beach. That's their creation story, the crawl from the mud of anonymity to the bright lights of stardom. Bruce Springsteen is from New Jersey. Johnny Carson was from

Nebraska. David Letterman is from Indiana. Paul McCartney is from Liverpool. Eminem is from Detroit. Sometimes that's all you ever hear. Other times, something iconic will appear. Mop tops for the Beatles. Steve Martin's white hair. Johnny Carson's golf club. Madonna's wardrobe. Prince's formerly-known-as ankh. Rock group Kiss's masks. The vaudevillian's goofy plaid jacket. The rocker's V-shaped guitar. Jay Leno's jaw. Snoop Dog's sunglasses. Elvis's pelvis. Others stress finding some word or phrase that successfully catches attention. "Heeere's Johnny!" "I never get no respect." Hardly a celebrity exists without some sense of back story. She's from Dublin. He used to be on *Saturday Night Live.* He owns lots of cars. Often these efforts are random gropings, trying to find the special ingredient that sparks public imagination. Trying to engineer their own success, managers and artists imitate pieces from the success of others. ("We need a new Steve McQueen.") But they are missing the complete code, the primal code.

Most marketers must reinvigorate themselves every few years. In some industries, every decade will do. Yet actors and rock stars are forced to continually reexcite and even reinvent themselves in order to sustain popular appeal. Madonna, for example, took the art of reinvention to a new level as she rebooted herself every eighteen to twenty-four months. Whether or not you enjoyed her permutations as Material Girl, 1991's *In Bed with Madonna* (she was after all, only *like* a virgin), or Eva Perón, Madonna has performed virtually every iteration to the tune of gold- and platinum-plus record sales. That's a track record that would turn traditional brand managers into comparative wimps. It's sort of like introducing an iPod ten times, or introducing a new Mini Cooper every other year to raging success.

In a business obsessed with equal parts youth, fashion, and rock 'n' roll, the business of staying in the music business has some sour notes. Many acts are one-hit wonders; few groups have a lifespan of more than a few years. Groups like the Rolling Stones, B. B. King, and Eric Clapton create images that sustain over time.

U2 is one such band. After twenty-five years and fourteen Grammys, U2 is bigger than ever. In marketing terms, their product life cycle is still on the upward curve.

The U2 ur-myth begins in 1976, when drummer Larry Mullen wanted to form a band. He picked four school friends from Mount Temple Comprehensive School in Dublin. "Larry formed U2," says Paul McGuinness, U2's manager from the beginning. "He auditioned the other three and he chose them. The first name of U2 was the Larry Mullen band," McGuinness laughs. "And he never lets us forget it."

The other members were and still are: Paul Hewson (Bono), Adam Clayton, and Dave Evans (The Edge). They bounced between, in McGuinness's words "two lousy names" —Feedback and The Hype—until they finally asked a friend who worked in an ad agency to come up with a better name for the group. Art director Steve Averill came up with a list, which included the name U2. It was more than a good name. "They instantly recognized that, apart from every-thing else, it was a graphic," says McGuinness. "You could put it on a poster and it immediately looked liked the biggest thing on the poster."

The logotype was automatically inclusive and became an

incredible icon. The band quickly seized the roles of rock stars. "We realized pretty early on that it would be pathetic to be good at the music and bad at the business. The corny old stories about artists getting fucked over didn't really appeal to us," says McGuinness. The band took control of the photography sessions and the music video shoots, realizing early on that the alternative to looking good in a photograph was, in Guinness's words, to look like shit. The effort paid off, and when articles on the band started showing up in magazines (and on thirteen *Rolling Stone* covers), they were accompanied by images shot by great photographers. And then there is Bono, the sleek, sexy, dynamic front man whose voice and aura has helped propel the group.

"In many ways," suggests McGuinness, "the greatest entertainers were intuitively able to resolve this big complex equation of art, money, sex, and politics. All these things collide. Somebody like Elvis Presley or Frank Sinatra or Bono is intuitively able to reduce this equation and produce excitement. When it really works, you *know*."

The music evolved, too. The undulating riptide of The Edge's guitar work became recognized and envied, an iconic sound that lets you know U2 is in the house. Through albums like *Joshua Tree, Achtung Baby,* and *All That You Can't Leave Behind* the band's music matured and grew fresh audiences.

The rituals in rock 'n' roll are the stuff of legend. From Jimi burning his guitar to Townsend's smashing his Telecaster, to the obligatory lit cigarette lighters, mosh pits, and mud slides, the *act* of rock has become as important as the music. U2 has been an incredible live act from the beginning, and while young bands usually start out by opening up for headliners, U2 rejected the notion of being anyone's warm-up act.

"From the very early days of U2 we played our own shows," says McGuinness. "We didn't like opening for other artists. We had a feeling, an intuition, that it would be better to play for a couple hundred people who had come to see U2 rather than play for a few thousand who had come to see some other band on the off chance they might like us.

"The other instinct we had from the beginning was, if we went into a city, we never overplayed. We wanted that city to know it was sold out. In a way, we've done that ever since." It's a modern twist on the old showbiz adage to always leave the audience begging for more. "At the moment," says McGuinness, "most of my time is spent managing the difficulties of underplaying every market in the world." He pauses. "Customers think it's unfair if they can't get a ticket, but the reality is we simply cannot supply the demand."

The other ritual of rock, of course, is creating the music. Their first album took three weeks to produce. *How to Dismantle an Atomic Bomb,* released in 2004, took a year and a half. "I can't believe they spend months chipping away at this big piece of rock and a year later there's a record there," says McGuinness. "I don't have a musical bone in my body. So when I go down to the studio to see them, I do not find the process of making records even remotely interesting," he grins. "I take care of business."

Even before the CD is finished in the studio, the hype machine revs into gear. The budgets for record companies are fractions of those allowed soft drink and car companies, so the music business historically has relied on garnering sound bites first from music audiences on radio and music television and from the music business press. Sometimes they can attach themselves to a movie, like U2 has done with *Batman, Mission Impossible,* and *Tomb Raider,* a process that McGuinness likens to their little tug attaching itself to an aircraft carrier. The rest of music marketing traditionally has been the endless slog of trying to inject buzz in the press. "The essence of marketing in the music business is parasitic," says McGuinness. "We can't advertise. The budgets in record companies are trivial, so how music is marketed is through radio and editorial, rarely through bought media."

Then along came Apple. "Getting involved with Apple," says McGuinness, "has been one of the most interesting things that we've ever done. Because the Apple people are brilliant. They are slightly cultish, but it's not an unhealthy cult."

U2 had many lucrative offers from advertisers over the years, but always turned them down. In spring 2002, however, Steve Jobs called asking for a meeting. His iTunes product was running into trouble. Major music stars were withholding their consent to download individual tracks on iTunes, declaring their music could only be loaded by the album. Steve Jobs was in search of a major artist to support his position. "I thought, well, of *course,* this is self-evident," says McGuinness. The music industry was in another major slump, and if people wanted to buy three songs rather than an entire CD, it was better than buying nothing. "Apple just invented the penicillin for our industry," says McGuinness. "I thought, Anyone who doesn't help them is an idiot."

At one meeting, Edge asked Steve Jobs if the iPod could be preloaded with the U2 catalog. That question started the process that resulted in the sexy black-and-red U2 Special Edition iPod that sells for about fifty dollars more than the ordinary unit (the iPod U2 is not loaded with U2 songs when you buy it). "They didn't pay us any money for the association," McGuinness confides. "They pay us a royalty on every U2 iPod."

Then some interesting things happened. Ordinarily, months or years might go by before people tire of hearing a hit song. Yet research from the radio stations was reporting that people were tired of hearing the first single on the U2 CD, a track titled "Vertigo." Explanation: Apple had supported their iPod introduction with a multimillion-dollar advertising campaign featuring U2 performing "Vertigo" pushed with real advertising dollars (McGuinness claims about $30 million supported the Apple iPod effort); U2's song was maxing out. The burnout took only a few weeks. "That almost never happens," nods McGuinness.

Today, U2 is defying gravity. Let's put that statement into context. U2's *How to Dismantle an Atomic Bomb* global tour will rake in over $300 million. (Projected figures by the music press for Elton John's 2005 tour are under $40 million.) "They are as ambitious and as hardworking and as tough-minded about what they do now as they were at the beginning," says McGuinness. "If anything, they work harder than when they were kids. From their point of view, we are the titleholders, we are the champions. If someone wants to be the champion, they have to take it away from us. They are very competitive in that respect."

The success of a rock and roll band, as Paul McGuinness says, is a mixture of art, money, sex, and politics. When they combine in the right mix, success happens. Sometimes.

The question arises, Can you make your own luck in the competitive world of show business? Certainly, talent is a huge issue. But many talented performers fail to get the sizzle or the acclaim that lesser talents sometimes do. Bottom line, the notes of primal code are firmly in place for U2. The creation story is a band from Dublin, blessed with a name that is inclusively iconic. The band looked hot and they played hot. Like Mick Jagger and other front men before him, lead singer Bono became the leader and an icon in his own right. Edge's guitar sound is also iconic. By forming their own private concert venue, they made the ritual live performances unique—the fact that they were often sold out also made them more desirable.

They created names for themselves—Bono, The Edge, which made them edgier—and with the song lyrics became the sacred words. The pagans, of course, were other bands. The U2 creed is a mutual embrace between becoming the world's greatest band and, faced with their current success, doing what it takes to stay on top. A pattern like the primal code cannot replace the magic that happens when four friends start playing music together. But without those pieces of code, no matter how good the music is it becomes an entirely different arrangement. Would U2 be as successful without the pieces of primal code in place? It is a question that cannot be answered, but must be asked. U2 manager Paul McGuinness sums it up: "We are very intuitive. Sometimes the process of examining disturbs the magic. Like conjurers or magicians, we do not explain the trick, even if we knew how."

Martha Stewart is a personality brand. Originally from New Jersey, Martha operated a catering service in Westport, Connecticut. Certainly, Martha was a caterer to the stars, but there are lots of caterers to the stars in Westport. (Westport and environs is home to Paul Newman, Keith Richards, David Letterman, Harvey Weinstein, and others.) So why are Martha's peers and competitors still whipping smoked trout mousse while Martha is a billionaire? Let's turn to the primal code.

Martha's creation story is well known. Born a Nutley, New Jersey, girl named Martha Kostyra, she spent time as a model, married a guy named Andrew Stewart, and moved to Westport, Connecticut. They bought an 1804 farmhouse and Martha started a successful catering business from her home. Martha wrote articles for *Family Circle* magazine on cooking, etiquette, gardening, and home arts, and in 1990 started her own magazine, called *Martha Stewart Living,* the beginning of her multimedia platform.

"Magazines usually didn't think of themselves as brands in this way," says New York designer Robert Valentine, who redesigned *Martha Stewart Living.* "They're not developing anything else beyond this *thing.*" According to Valentine, Martha was one of the first to think beyond the magazine. "She had the products, she had the catalog; most magazines don't do that," he notes. (When *Martha Stewart Living* first appeared, the word "lifestyle" wasn't even a part of popular vocabulary.)

That same year, Martha penned a hardcover book on how to organize and create *Weddings*. Ironically, she and her husband filed for divorce that same year. The success of *Weddings* was followed by a cookbook, more books followed, and her own television shows went on the air.

For thirty minutes each week Martha became an icon, as she showed how even ordinary women could lead a good, elegant life. It didn't matter if she was preparing a French recipe or tying a ribbon on a box, everything Martha did was a ritual of joy. It was, as she put it, "a good thing." In 1999, she started Martha Stewart Living Omnimedia. Of course, Martha's pursuit of perfection led to critics and nonbelievers. Her pretensions sat poorly with some; she put herself on a pedestal that had to be knocked down. Even so, when Martha's stock went public in 1999, she became a billionaire. Her company suffered when she became involved in a stock scandal. Nevertheless, Martha is still "a good thing."

Oprah Gail Winfrey is also a primal personality. Virtually everyone in the United States is aware of how Oprah was raised on a farm in Mississippi and served as the first African-American newscaster at Nashville's WTVF-TV. She moved to Baltimore where, by her own admission, she broke down crying during the live broadcast of a report on a fire that destroyed a family home. Management was not pleased with her nonobjective journalism, and she wound up in Chicago, hosting a morning talk show at a Chicago television station. It was there that her star began its rise. Within the year, in 1984, the inauspicious *AM Chicago* morning show turned into *The Oprah Winfrey Show*. Oprah had finally landed her form of communication. Over time, Oprah revealed that she had been sexually abused by an older cousin at the age of nine. That, and her chronic weight issues, gave her an empathy and vulnerability that made her the Every-woman among talk-show hosts.

Her struggle to find her own place within the male-dominated world of broadcast television and surmount the black woman's place in society has never been easy. But she has succeeded beyond what anyone might have imagined. *The Oprah Winfrey Show* is watched by millions. She has received numerous awards. And she is one of a select group of women in film and television to own her production studio.

If Oprah has a creed, it is about self-determination and personal growth. "Not living my life to please other people," she is quoted in one interview, "but doing what my heart says all the time. That's the biggest lesson for me. It's very difficult for me to even see myself as successful because I still see myself as in the process of becoming successful." Seeing herself as a work in process is one thing that gives Oprah her vulnerability and ultimate humanity. She is a compulsive learner. And because she has been hurt, she has learned how to turn pain into precious mental real estate.

In an address to Wellesley graduates, Oprah counseled, "Turn your wounds into wisdom. You will be wounded many times in your life. You'll make mistakes. Some people will call them failures, but I have learned that failure is really God's way of saying, 'Excuse me, you're moving in the wrong direction.' It's just an experience, just an experience."

Like most personalities, Oprah herself is the icon. According to Marketing Evaluations The Q Scores Company, 90 percent of the public know who Oprah is. Her Q score (a mathematic equation of recognition and likability) is 31. The average Q score is a 15. But Oprah is not the only icon. Her imagery includes satellite icons that include *The Oprah Winfrey Show,* the Oprah Book Club, and *O* magazine.

The ritual of turning on the television set to watch *The Oprah Winfrey Show* is a daily rite for over 20 million people in 132 countries. Each show is a ceremony of lights, music, and drama. Recently, Oprah added some horsepower to the daily ritual when she waved her hand and gave her studio audience three hundred Pontiac G6 automobiles. The stunt earned priceless publicity, and Oprah followed up with other giveaway flourishes. As part of her efforts for education, when women started organizing informal book clubs, Oprah started Oprah's Book Club. All forty-six books she recommended became best-sellers.

Oprah's repeated diets over the years have also become mini rites as, like millions of women in her audience, she alternately loses and regains her weight. But it is Oprah's ultimate warmth and compassion that draws viewers everywhere. Her philanthropy extends from her Angel Network, and includes everything from providing educational programs and scholarships to promoting community volunteerism to Habitat for Humanity (a project in which she wants to build a home in each of the over two hundred markets she is viewed in).

The soundtrack of virtually any show creates sacred words, because ultimately Oprah is about life. How to keep it, how to live it, how to survive it, how to become happy with it. It is probably expected that the show that created Dr.

Phil would be filled with words that are meaningful for her audience. Here are just a few.

- If you can learn to focus on what you have, you will always see that the universe is abundant and you will have more.
- When people show you who they are, believe them, the first time.
- Create the highest, grandest vision possible for your life because you become what you believe.

Oprah is so universally loved that it is doubtful that even her talk-show competitors would wish her harm. If there are pagans or nonbelievers, they are on the fringe. There are occasional outbursts, like the Beef Council, but they are rare. They are the child abusers, racists, and misogynists who decry the advancement of women and people of color. There are others, of course, who are against the populist appeal of daytime television and even against the concept of television itself. They are all in the minority.

The leader of this primal personality is undeniably Oprah. In every sense, she runs her own show. She is CEO of her production company, the Harpo Entertainment Group, and its subsidiaries. She is quoted as saying that "it wasn't until I was demoted as an on-air anchor woman and thrown into the talk-show arena to get rid of me that I allowed my own truth to come through. The first day I was on the air doing my first talk show back in 1978, it felt like breathing, which is what your true passion should feel like. It should be so natural to you. And so, I took what had been a mistake, what had been perceived as a failure with my career as an anchor woman in the news business and turned it into a talk-show career that's done OK for me!"

Oprah's Q scores are higher today than they have been in years. The key to Oprah's talent has been her credo of accessibility and vulnerability. In the end, she has become a friend, the kind of friend that millions of people around the world invite into their homes every day.

You can apply the pattern of primal branding to other celebrities like David Letterman, Jay Leno, the President of the United States, Michael Moore, Walter Cronkite, and the hundreds and thousands of others who seep into our popular gestalt. There is a reason beyond talent that gives them an aura in our consciousness and helps them rise above the mass of other talented figures.

Even the enduring genius of Mozart can be examined in terms of the primal code. Everyone reading this will know Mozart's abilities as a performer and composer at an early age (his creation story). His creed, of course, was his genius. His brilliance. Or, as fellow composer Franz Joseph Hayden said, "He has taste." Mozart's icons then, as now, were not the plaster busts we see perched on top of pianos, but his compositions. The rituals were performances of his work by himself in his own time and by others today. The name "Mozart" is itself a sacred word in the world of classical music. Of course, his music also takes on the characteristics of the sacred in his over forty symphonies, and in his operas, including *Don Giovanni, Cosi fan tutte,* and *The Marriage of Figaro.* Mozart's other works include piano concertos, piano sonatas, violin sonatas, string quartets, chamber works, and serenades. Mozart was a genius, and his work will probably always be played. But his sustained popularity (there's a classical radio station in L.A. called K-MOZART) may be in part because of the construct of primal code that is woven through Mozart's story. Suffice it to say that we know less of Dvořák, Liszt, or Tchaikovsky (and perhaps we hear less of them, too).

On the westbound I-94 in St. Paul, Minnesota, just north of the Vandalia exit, a scowling face plastered on the side of a water tower glares down over the freeway as if judging puzzled passersby.

The creation of artist Shepard Fairey, the scowling OBEY GIANT icon is part of a phenomenology campaign that has been spotted by unwitting millions in cities from New York City to Tokyo to Berlin. As a brand practitioner and self-proclaimed "world heavyweight champion propagandist," Fairey is someone who created a brand *before* he had a product. For this reason, the former underground art student is sometimes a consultant for marketers like Coca-Cola. Because Fairey has successfully attracted the hard-to-connect under-thirty age segment—the group bombarded with over 14.6 million advertising impressions by the time they reach age twenty—marketers are eager to find out the what and how of his anti-ad success.

Fairey's experiment in phenomenology started fifteen years ago, while a student at Rhode Island School of Design. "I had a friend over, and he wanted to learn how to make a stencil, and I was looking through the newspaper and came across this wrestling ad for Andre the Giant, and I said, 'Hey, why don't you do this?'" Thinking that the wrestling image wasn't cool enough, the friend resisted. Fairey was irked. As a senior member of the surf skateboard graffiti scene, he found himself becoming irritated with the relentless, often pathetic quest for coolness. His answer was Hegelian: anti-cool.

"I said, 'No man, you gotta do this Andre thing,'" says Fairey. " 'It's awesome. That's the new posse. Andre's posse is the new thing.' It was a spontaneous joke, a sarcastic commentary on our world. And he was like, 'Hey, yeah, we won't tell anyone who it is.' That was the spark of it."

Fairey created a poster that read "Andre The Giant Has A Posse." He pasted posters around the art school and the city of Providence. What he thought would be a joke turned into a phenomenon. "When you put something up in the public space and it's unexplained, people want to know what it is, and they ask, What is this thing? They don't want to be the last one to know."

Not only was Fairey fascinated by people's responses, but he also felt empowered. "No one knew it was me," says Fairey. "But I knew, and therefore I felt like my existence was validated. I just thought, if I was creating buzz with this little effort, what if I actually put real effort into it?" Fairey took his mission from Providence to Boston, then to New York.

Over time, Fairey started "bombing" (the term graffiti artists use for putting their images in public spaces) cities across the country and around the planet. Giant posters appeared in Tokyo, London, Paris, Hong Kong, Melbourne,

Osaka, Berlin, Copenhagen, Oslo—even at the Aztec ruins in Tulum, Mexico.

Fairey's mission of "manufacturing quality dissent" has evolved over the last decade and a half. "I did the original 'Andre has a posse' sticker, then I did Andre as a head." Then Andre as Jimi Hendrix, Andre as Gene Simmons, then Peter Max style. "I did a lot of pop culture references with it," says Fairey. "I was pretty much hijacking anything of pop culture resonance." Today, Fairey's studio manufactures posters and stickers, and licenses clothing bearing the Giant and other images like his Big Brother "icon face."

Wherever OBEY GIANT lies aesthetically, where the image presents itself on the street is usually against the law. Fairey stalks the empty city streets armed with a bucket of wheat paste and paper posters under his arm. Pasted on street poles, on utility company boxes, the sides of buildings, empty billboards, or glued over outdoor advertisements, Giant postings are often illegal. Fairey's first postings were a political act against the floating world of popular commercialism and complacency. "A lot of people feel like they need rules to feel stable. I feel like I need to bend the rules to feel stable," quips the culture-jamming street artist. "I do what I do because I want to do it. Because it satisfies me for some reason."

Fairey's bombing runs have become rituals in themselves. Although he prefers to travel alone or only with one other person, today he often finds himself accompanied by zealous art followers and a film crew. "Now people always want to go and photograph and film me," says Fairey. "People like to feel like they were capturing it while it was happening. I've had to decline a lot of that, because it attracts attention."

A story from the Shepard Fairey legend. "These very wealthy guys from Japan decided they liked my art and flew me to Japan for my very first art show in Japan and opened a store for me that was carrying my products," tells Fairey. "When I was in Japan, they would go out and put up posters with me, they got such a rush out of it. And there's this huge department store right in Shabuya called Sabu which, while I was in Japan, had this blank billboard on the side of it. And it was right at rush hour when the street is wall-to-wall people." Fairey brazenly climbed up to the billboard and pasted his images onto the empty board. In the center of Tokyo. In the middle of rush-hour traffic. The Japanese videotaped the whole event. "They were just so crazy about that. They kept watching the video footage over and over and showing all their friends. All you could see was my extension pole going up with the glue going on. You couldn't see me because there were so many people. You could see like half the Giant face go up and then more glue and then the other half of the face go up, and then I'd go back across the street with my bucket and they're going nuts."

When his Japanese backers came to L.A., they wanted to go out again.

"I said, Oh yeah, there's this one billboard on the 101 freeway that's blank that I want to get. They said, Can we watch? I knew how much pleasure they got out of it when we were in Japan. I thought, Yeah sure," says Fairey. "The next thing I know, they've called all the other guys in the L.A. office on their cell phones and we've got five cars caravanning over there. Definitely more than I wanted. I thought it was going to be more like two cars or one car. But I didn't have the heart to tell them no. Statistically, I get away with it more often than I get caught, so I thought, This isn't ideal, but I'll bring them.

"So we go to this spot in Echo Park right near the Ramparts Police Station and it's kind of a shady neighborhood. We park. I climb over the fence. I do the billboard. They go and stand on the other side of the street and watch. When I'm finished, I climb back out, and I put my ladder in the car. The bucket of wheat paste is still sitting on the sidewalk. We're all just standing on the sidewalk and saying our goodbyes when a cop car speeds by. Then another cop car speeds by. Then two more stop right in front of us, and the other cars flip around and then the helicopter is there.

"I guess someone had seen me climbing over the fence and thought that I was breaking into a building. Eventually, there are six cop cars there and a helicopter and they line us all up against the wall and tell us to spread out. My wife, Amanda, is at one end, I'm toward the other end, and I'm telling all the people on either side of me to let me do all the talking. All the Japanese pretend they didn't speak English. I was too far away from Amanda to coordinate the story with her, but luckily the billboard was facing the freeway. On the side of the billboard from where we were standing was an ad, on the other side was my image. But the cops couldn't see that.

"They asked, What are you doing over here? And I said, Oh, well, these are patrons of mine from Japan who I do a clothing line with and we were all eating and they were going to follow us back to our warehouse but we were on the freeway together and we lost them so we took the next exit and told them to take that exit so we could all join back up and then keep going. And so now we're just reconvening and getting ready to go.

"They didn't look in my car. They didn't question a bucket of wheat paste. They talked to Amanda, and Amanda miraculously gave basically the same story.

"They just let us go and they left," says Fairey.

"But the Japanese guys were so amazed by the whole experience. Like, I'm sure they've seen Ice Cube videos on MTV or something, but this was like, the real deal. They wouldn't have liked it if they had gone to jail, but they liked that story."

Jail time seems to have become a ritual unto itself. Incarcerated eleven times, the thirty-five-year-old Fairey shows no signs of letting up. Perhaps he is committed to the political act of defaming complacency. Perhaps he is addicted to the adrenaline rush and the act of not getting caught. When was the last time he went on a bombing run? A pause. "Week and a half ago," he admits.

Fairey's work is as insistent as it is provocative. His original command, OBEY, is a reverse directive, asking people to question first, then act. "I chose the word 'obey' because I thought it would be good to get people to question their obedience, and what better way than to confront them with the idea of obeying something. Now, *what* am I supposed to obey?" Like most things underground, Shepard Fairey's work found its way aboveground, where he found a waiting audience. Fairey's street buzz spread into the commercial world. His first studio, BLK/MRKT and his newest company, Studio Number One, have been helping marketers like

Sunkist, Express jeans, Red Bull, and the music group Black-Eyed Peas. Straddling the worlds of gangster graffiti and corporate boardrooms, Fairey has grossed over $1 million helping the commercial industry. The irony is pragmatic. The corporate money funds Fairey's guerilla art to paper the streets.

After fifteen years of experimenting with phenomenology, what does it all mean? "One of the things that I've concluded is, people project whatever wishful thinking onto things they have," says Fairey. "Such as, I'm likely to win the lottery, but I'm not likely to get cancer from smoking. That's been interesting."

Another thing.

"People take ownership of images and define themselves through that. Fashion is a total reflection of that. Just because something is new, and I'm one of the few people who have it, that makes me superior. Once it becomes too common, then it becomes not cool. Some people are consoled by the idea that they have something that everyone else has, and that actually makes them feel like they belong. And then the trendsetters, like, they don't want to have anything that everybody else has, and they want to move along from that, and that dynamic is very fascinating." And, finally. "If you can supply something that stimulates conspicuous consumption, you can create something from nothing. And that's what a world capitalist society is about. You can't just rely on people consuming gasoline and food—the necessities. In order for the economy to thrive, you have to rely on conspicuous consumption being stimulated."

Fairey's success can be related to the relevance of his anti-image image during the 1990s consumer fever. But the relationship he has with his followers strikes much deeper. Fairey has created a belief system around his iconic communications. His creation story as a young art student who unwittingly discovers his Eureka! moment; his Giant and icon face icons; his ritualistic bombing runs; his credo of manufacturing (and distributing) quality dissent against the white-washed pillars of conformist, complacent consumerism; his sacred words like "OBEY", "bombing," "phenomenology," and others. Fairey has cracked the code on how to create a community of people who consume his work, no matter where they are on the planet. They believe in what Shepard Fairey is about, and are willing to spend millions to prove one incontrovertible truth.

Shepard Fairey Has A Posse.

PART THREE

The
Final Step

6. Primal Reengineering

Primal branding is an organizing principle to help products, services, personalities, and civic communities achieve popular appeal. Many outstanding books and articles have been written about branding. A few even allude to the existence of brand tribes, brand cults, and communities: *The Culting of Brands: When Customers Become True Believers,* by Douglas Atkin; *Lovemarks: The Future Beyond Brands,* by Kevin Roberts; *How Brands Become Icons: The Principles of Cultural Branding,* by Douglas B. Holt; *Adcult USA,* by James B. Twitchell; *The New Culture of Desire,* by Melinda Davis; and *New Brand World,* by Scott Bedbury are among the best works on the existence of cultural brands. Seth Godin's *Permission Marketing,* and *Built to Last* by Jim Collins offer other terrific insights.

While brain researchers watch our lobes light up like Christmas trees when we experience love, bliss, and brands we admire, we have not discovered how to create that brand love. We stand by and watch other brands resonate in ways we wish we could. As the manager of one famous brand remarked, "We don't know how we were able to create what we have created, we just know that we don't want to screw it up."

As we have seen, the failure of brands to gain real emotive power is due to the fact that they have relied on only one or two components of the primal code to communicate their brand message. The goal is to wrap all seven pieces of code around the messaging to create a fully functioning community of believers.

Just as the primal code can be revealed in hindsight, it can be implemented with foresight. The seven pieces of primal code are a map—or checklist—that can help guide your efforts to create a brand that people can believe in. It is a movement from unknowing to knowing.

Primal branding is a simple way to decode the intangible power behind brands. In workshops called Primal Digs, we work together with companies to help them engineer and reverse engineer their brands and their company culture. The primal code is a language, like genetic code or computer code. We help companies learn the vernacular of primal branding, by first explaining the seven pieces of code. Then they explore which pieces already exist in their company and brand(s), and which pieces are absent or have grown stale and tired. Too often, pieces of code are missing. People have forgotten or discarded their creation story (for example, when Smirnoff recently went back and discovered their origins, it gave them incentive to go on to become the world's best-selling vodka). Some business people have not identified or do not understand the significance of their rituals. Even consumer electronics companies like Samsung and Best Buy, for example, understand today that how people relate to their products during the shopping rite is not just a feature-driven experience. Samsung is experimenting with the use of scent at its Samsung Experience proto-facility on Columbus Circle in New York City to keep people inside the store longer. And Best Buy is designing its store experiences around consumer-centric desires. Each customer visit or phone call by your sales department is a significant ritual that can be modeled into a more resonant experience by providing surprising new products, new information, and relevant news into what might otherwise be a complacent, routine event. Most firms are aware of the relevance of their logo as an icon, but fail to recognize that their storefronts, headquarters building, product design, even the smell of their stores, hotel lobbies, or airport concourses are equally iconic. Many firms still haven't figured out their company creed, or a statement that declares what they are all about.

We also work with companies to determine the best ways to plug in the missing pieces of code, or how to bring freshness and energy to pieces that have been neglected. Once we have all of the pieces of code in place, we plan best processes for keeping them continually refreshed. A common mistake is for companies to think that once everything is in place, they can check it off as a brand well done. But no brand that intends to resonate with its consumer lies fallow. Brands are active engagements that continually reboot themselves to keep the consumer wondering what's going to happen next. Target stores change their shelves every three months, to invigorate the shopping ritual. Starbucks always has new product offerings and new experiences to intensify customer's ritual visits. We have already seen how Campbell's soup, for example, continually refreshes their iconic package.

The methods of implementing primal branding are as

varied as the company and the situation. As marketing prac-
titioners are aware, real world next-steps depend upon the
industry, the company, the market environment and competitive pressures. Great minds do not think alike. And if all we
needed were a recipe, everyone would be a great chef. Knowing the power and vibrancy of the seven pieces of primal
code, however, becomes a unifying principle to help guide
you and other members of your group toward engineering a
more vibrant and competitive brand. The basic act of ensur-
ing all pieces of code are in place, for example, in itself creates
powerful brand resonance. Continually tweaking, revitaliz-
ing, and implementing the pieces of code lets you manage the
intangible emotional components of your product, service,
individual, or community, and attracts people who want to
believe.

The act of engineering—or re-engineering—a brand
involves not just marketing officers, but the chief executive
officer, product designers, as well as people in human
resources, manufacturing, innovation, technology, marketing communications, media, and other departments. It must
be determined, for example, who needs to communicate the
creation story (should it be in advertising, on the website, in
the annual report, information for new hires, on the packaging, in the lobby?). Tasks for the other pieces of code also
become aligned with proper individuals and departments.

Great kinships develop during this process, and the effect
is psychologically robust. It is not unusual for people exposed
to the primal process during Primal Digs to bond in ways
that inadvertently exclude those who do not attend. For that
reason, the director of one company actually hired an office

temp to take over the switchboard, so that the receptionist could attend a Primal Dig. The result is a switched-on group committed to propelling the ideals and mission of the brand. Ultimately, everyone is responsible for the brand.

Another facet of primal branding seems obvious now, but was initially unexpected. While most companies strive to attract large groups of consumers, clients, customers, and guests, the primal code also works at a micro level to create smaller groups. Sales teams or project teams, for example, can also be bonded together to achieve a common goal using primal techniques. The creation story would be the how and why this special group is being brought together. The creed might be to increase sales in the Northeast region, target a new client, or program new software by a certain deadline. IBM re-engineered its Big Blue sales teams from product groups by giving them an overarching creed called *e-business*. The icons might be the deadline timetable or, in the case of new product innovation, the product itself might become the icon. The Volkswagen Beetle and Mini Cooper automobiles became vibrant totems for the project teams who worked on them. Working 24/7 shifts, status meetings, and sales calls become rituals with great importance to the team. The way you approach new business is rarely the way you look at a routine sales call. Sacred words spring up spontaneously in demanding situations like these. Names like "Project Blue" and "Team Birmingham" pop up, differentiating this primal group—and their mission—from the rest of the organization. Slogans that chant your mission become sacred words, as do phrases like "Programming is much better than having a social life," and "This is a great place to work, if your parents can afford to send you here." Humor and irony become release mechanisms in these demanding, pressure-cooker environments. As the team builds esprit, pagans become anyone outside the team (sometimes even upper management), for the bond created within the primal group cannot be underestimated. Remember the Marine Corps. The surround of primal code leads men and women into battle as easily as charging onto the sales floor. Their zeal, of course, is exactly what you want to accomplish the task. Damn the torpedoes. The leader of the team is the individual who carries the vision, the person who sets out against all odds to redefine the world—whether that be through product innovation, a new dimension in computer programming, researching a DNA strand, or driving sales in a new territory. Importantly, he or she is also the person responsible for implementing the primal code.

The aspect of team creation—and creating true believers within the team—is a critical and welcome benefit of primal branding. And as useful for sales and marketing teams as it is for product innovation teams, software developers, medical research groups, architects and their engineering counterparts, new product S.W.A.T. teams, marketing folk, and baseball teams.

Sometimes when I explain primal branding, executives nod their heads and say, "Oh sure, we have every one of those things." Yet if you asked the ordinary consumer, they would reply they don't feel any vibrancy or connection to that brand. Why? The usual reason is that they really don't have all of the pieces of code. Or managers haven't communicated the pieces of code to the public as well as they think. This is typical brand boosterism, when brand leaders think consumers care as much about their brands as they do.

The first step in primal branding is to determine where your brand exists in the minds of customers. Many companies already have customer information they can sort to determine how their brand aligns with the primal code and consumers. A brand audit can help you define which pieces of code you need to develop or focus on. You can do this by looking at each piece of code to see how it relates to your company, personality, product, or industry. The following pages will help you decide what questions to ask yourself, and give you some next steps for moving forward. Sometimes the brand's primal elements need tweaking—the icons need to be updated, the creed needs to be defined, rituals enhanced, more pronounced leadership, better deliberate communication of the elements in media. Sometimes a top-to-bottom restructuring is necessary.

When General Motors decided to rebrand its GMC truck and SUV line, they needed to extricate themselves from Chevrolet. Until a few years ago there was no distinction between the two General Motors products. When consumers looked at a GMC on the sales floor, they were fundamentally looking at a Chevrolet with a GMC logo. (Both divisions, for example, sold the oversized Suburban and forced customers to decide for themselves if they wanted the Chevrolet-branded Suburban or GMC-branded Suburban. Naturally, Chevrolet took the lion's share.) GMC evolved its creed around engineering. Its new advertising tag line—"We are professional grade"—reflected the change. GMC distanced itself from the muddier-than-thou Chevy truck rural America image with clean steel and urban iconography. With a more aggressive grille, refined headlamps, and other design details the iconography of the vehicles was also transformed, and GMC is still evolving.

How did your company or idea start? Who started it? Did it start because someone was frustrated, because the marketplace was changing, because someone had a dream? *Where* did it start—was it an idea two guys came up with on an airplane, did someone see a crack in the marketplace, did someone have an insight while on vacation? These are actual examples of inspiration. Whether the idea started in a hotel room, a garage, or borrowed space, it is important back story. Often, the story of how the company started is so well known to old hands at the company that they assume everyone is aware of it and they neglect to inform new employees, new managers, new hires of every stripe. During one primal branding workshop, we asked a twenty-year veteran of TIES, an educational technology company, to stand up and recite the story of the company's history from its beginnings half a century earlier to the present. When he finished, we asked for a show of hands of how many people knew that story. About half. This happens inside many long-established companies and results in a fractured culture, with people who were there in the beginning and have internalized what the company is about, while everyone else (managers included) stumble along. Thankfully, TIES management took steps to rectify their dilemma. Every company was started some-where, somehow, by someone. The origin story is the begin-ning of the brand narrative, the start of the mission. Whether your company was started in a garage, on the back of a paper napkin, or by companies merging together, that story is vitally important.

A friend was competing for fresh MBA graduates at an international holding company. As CEO, she realized these young prospects were hungry for international experience (she offered none). She also realized that her company was probably the least sexy of those in the company's portfolio. Desperate, she decided to try the primal code. With each applicant, she outlined how her company began and what it was about, showed the products as icons, how she influenced rituals, and outlined the competitive set. (Of course, she didn't say, "And here are my rituals . . ."; it was an informal but carefully outlined discussion.) A week later, a dazed human resources manager stepped into her office. "They all want to work for you," he exclaimed.

When companies merge to form the Bank Ones, Verizons, and Altria Groups of the world the origin story needs to be rebooted around the new corporate vision. People within the merged enterprise need a fresh starting point. The refreshed creation story helps coworkers, vendors, and customers awaken to a new dawn charged with bright new opportunities.

Where the creation story is told is also important. The story of how two guys named Bartles & Jaymes started a wine-cooler company was a complete fiction, embellished in over one hundred television commercials. The story of two guys named Tom who started Nantucket Nectars by rowing groceries to the yachts in Nantucket Harbor is true and is on the label for everyone to see. Film director Quentin Tarantino's creation story about how he was a film geek who worked in a video rental store was retold over and over in the press. The story of how UPS started as a bike messenger company in Seattle is available on page one of the UPS Web site.

The importance of the creation story in our role as human beings should not be understated. As members of a United Nations burial detail uncovered a mass grave in the remote African bush they discovered a photo album squeezed among the dead bodies. Inside the album were snapshots of birthdays, grandparents, and family events. When the person lying dead in the mass grave was pulled from their home they grabbed the family album—the family story as told in pictures—and carried it with them. If you doubt the importance of the creation story within the human context, remember that photo album.

The creed is the second piece of code. Many companies have invested hundreds of man and woman hours unraveling the company mission and distilling their products and services, hopes and dreams into a succinct statement. Sometimes that statement can become the creed. Often, however, the mission statement satisfies other internal objectives. The creed should answer the question, Why do we belong in people's lives? Why do we come to work in the morning? Why should people care? The answer might be, To invent. To discover. To teach. To save. To discuss. To enlighten. What does your company celebrate? Is it precision quality? Breakthrough innovation? Best-of-class customer service? Incredible performance? Ecoeconomics?

What, after all, does your company believe in? Is it to design computers "for the rest of us" like Apple? Is it to make your experience the "third place" like Starbucks? Is it to make the widest number of products available online like amazon.com? Do you want to green the planet like Aveda and Stonyfield Farm? Or design safe automobiles like Volvo?

Hopefully, the creed will be a statement less obtuse than "Magic you can trust" or "Arrogance justified." Sometimes the creed can be the boiled-down word essence that drives the advertising.

Once written, the creed must be communicated. Sometimes, like Aveda, it is seen every day in the company lobby by employees and visitors. The creed is a part of daily operations like the UPS policy book. Or it is watched by millions on television commercials, like Saturn, HP, and FedEx. The opposite extreme is that the creed is buried in a corporate handbook or, worse, locked inside the entrepreneur or CEO's brain, leaving managers and coworkers to extract a sense of vision and purpose on their own. Worse, they import their prior employer's mission into the void.

When mergers occur, when companies are purchased by financial holding groups, the result can be a collision of differing creeds, disparate visions, different values, even opposing views on how best to create products and services. In the best scenarios potential conflicts can be clarified and resolved during due process.

When potential suitors looked at Stonyfield Farm, recalls CEO Gary Hirshberg, they recognized redundancies and automatically plotted overhead cuts in their minds. "What they weren't really owning up to is that 'overhead' is a euphemism for human beings," says Hirshberg. "So when Danone came along and said, 'We don't want to touch you, we want to leave you exactly as you are,' that's when I realized that's the kind of culture I could see investing in. The leadership that went into that judgment on their part had a vision of how Stonyfield could support their ultimate objectives."

Creeds must sometimes be updated. This happens naturally for companies like Motorola, which transformed their business from televisions to cellular technologies. The same held true for IBM and UPS as technologies and markets evolved.

The creed is a principle; it is what the company is about. "I think of brands as a promise to a customer," says Linda Berkeley, president of National Geographic Enterprises and executive vice president of National Geographic. "When somebody buys something with National Geographic on it, it says something about who they are and what we stand for. In a world that has multiplied the ways you reach people, and things happen so quickly and there's so much exposure, you have to be ever vigilant. You have so many consumer touchpoints. The responsibility is to make sure that in every way you are meeting the expectation of the consumer. I see that as a big responsibility."

The expression of what your product or service is about becomes concentrated and instantly communicated in your icons. The question people often have is, How can I tell what my icons are? As discussed elsewhere in this book, icons can be as simple as your company logo or as discreet as senses like taste or smell. Icons can be the product itself. Ask yourself, What are the Wham! moments when the senses are slammed by a concentration of meaning instantly identified with your brand? How does your brand make an impression? Is it the product? The experience? A look? A taste? A smell? What is the first impression? What is the last impression? Vibrant brands have many icons that propel the brand. Starbucks, for example, has their iconic mermaid logo. But they also have that white cup that can be spotted from across the street, the corrugated paper comfort ring, the green aprons, barrista counter, and wood and hued environments, all icons of the Starbucks experience.

The icon could be your building. It could be your brand experience: the entry into your retail store. The receptionist. The greeter. The smell as customers step inside. The water-fall in the lobby. The music you play (or don't play). If you're a personality brand it's your face, your hair (remember Andy Warhol), that space between your front teeth, the clothes you wear, your smile. If you're a civic community your icons might be your skyline or the bridge that crosses the river or the rose gardens or the square everyone congregates in. Or all of the above.

Shaping icons falls under the designing arts: graphic, product, and experience, plus sound and aroma, if you're interested. The more complex the brand engagement, the larger the army of designers and idea engineers that will be needed. Companies like Coca-Cola, General Motors, Target, Samsung, and Procter and Gamble have legions of talented people continually refreshing or rebooting the iconic expres-sions of their brand portfolios. It is a continual engagement.

"The classic example of this is Campbell's soup's red-and-white can," says Landor's Susan Nelson. "While people think that it has never changed, if you line them up you'll see that it is constantly being refreshed."

Davin Stowell at Smart Design reminds us that the product should be updated, too. When CorningWare and Pyrex first appeared in the 1950s they were all about innovation and technology. They were created from technology developed for missile nose cones, after all. Says Stowell, "They sold the product based on how it could improve things in the kitchen. You could use it on the range top, you could use it in the oven." According to Stowell, Corning spent time and money superficially promoting the brand but let the product itself stagnate. While the customer evolved, the product became a dinosaur. "My mom liked it," says Stowell, "but I don't know why I should buy it."

"In the 1950s, Betty Crocker was the Martha Stewart of her age," adds David Altshul of Character. "She had a radio show, she had cookbooks, she had dishware." In baby steps and over time General Mills made a series of decisions that devolved Betty Crocker into a character and a spoon. "And now they don't know what to do with her," says Altshul.

The longer a brand has been in existence, the more layered the icons become. For example, there is not just one icon for democracy United States–style. The icons run deep: the Stars and Stripes, Mount Rushmore, the Washington Monument, the voting booth, the Lincoln Memorial, the United States Capitol building, the Statue of Liberty, and more. For over two hundred years the same accumulation has occurred for the rituals, sacred words, leaders, and other pieces of code that create the brand called "U.S.A."

Don't forget that the entrance to your building, your store, your office is often your customer's first impression. While it seems extreme to compare the entrance of a Target, a Best Buy, or grocery store to Bernini's piazza at St. Peter's in Rome, lessons can be learned from architect Richard Meier's description: "The colonnades are like arms that enclose you and make you feel that this is an extraordinary space," he declares. How many retail stores make you feel that engaged?

People are often as confused about what constitutes a ritual as they are about icons. I have outlined many examples of rituals throughout this book. As a general guide, rituals are actions that involve how the product is used, how the service is engaged, where and how the consumer goes to shop, and how the product is maintained, returned, renewed, downloaded, or updated. One way of discerning the rituals involved with your product, service, person, or civic community is to think through how people become involved with your brand. Draw a timeline and write down the moment when people are first introduced to your brand (whether through word of mouth, a salesperson, or advertising), then the string of ritual events that follow: pulling into the store's parking lot, entering the store threshold, encountering the greeter, the ritual of walking through the aisles, what happens at checkout, then getting back in the car again.

Each of these actions is a repeated event that can entail positive or negative experiences. Determine which rituals might have negative effects and tweak or revamp them. If the store location is hard to get to (the bane of retail), it is a negative experience that should be seriously reconsidered. If the area surrounding the store is dirty and unwelcoming, then that is a part of the ritual of the store visit that needs improvement. If the greeter doesn't seem to care, if the aisles are narrow or poorly stocked or overstocked or poorly laid out, those are obstacles to a positive experience. If the checkout lines are too long, if the cashier is a dope, if the checkout technology is behind the times, they may need a redesign.

Consider a simple trip to the grocery store. At Stew Leonard's in Norwalk, Connecticut, shoppers walk through a loopy maze as mechanical bears dressed in farmers' overalls play banjos, someone dressed in a cow suit waves at infants, and visitors take children to a petting zoo in the store parking lot. Once shoppers ramble through this Disney-meets-grocery maze, another ritual is revealed. Random customers are rewarded with tokens for ice cream cones they can redeem at the dairy counter. On their way out of the store shoppers see snapshots of smiling customers holding up Stew Leonard's bags in Athens, London, Rome, Hawaii, and other distant locations.

These are all positive rituals encased in the ritual weekly trip to the grocery store that have embellished and heightened the mundane into something exciting. It's easy to see why Stew Leonard's has created a community spread around the globe from a not-so-simple grocery store on the Post Road in Norwalk, Connecticut.

As mentioned elsewhere, sales calls and telephone calls are also a ritual. If you want to hear a terrific phone experience, call Nike headquarters. If you want a poor experience, call your phone company or your bank. As an exercise, describe how you would make those rituals easier, more personal, and more rewarding. For example, do we really need to push our way through five layers of buttons only to have to repeat all of that same information again when we finally reach a human being?

Rituals can be positive or negative reinforcements of the brand. It's your job to determine which.

The pagans, or nonbelievers, are usually the easiest to identify. They are most often your competition, another way of working (think Mac versus PC), other ways of thinking ("supply and demand" versus "on-demand"). Who are you not? What are you trying to avoid? Who are you up against? While it is easy to set yourself up against the competitors that help differentiate you outside the company, it is more difficult—and painful—to identify the pagans within your organization. One software company was faced with people who couldn't attend to clients' software questions in a timely manner, resulting in lots of frustrated customers. In a primal session one of the people responsible for the slow service suddenly blurted out, "We're our own pagans."

Some companies live in fear of alienating potential customers by defining them as pagans, preferring to leave a door open. That does not deny the fact that you will always have people you aren't right for. They'll be there, anyway. By acknowledging them, you can respond to their needs and create new opportunities to engage them. Realizing years ago that not everyone wanted sugar-laden soft drinks, the beverage industry created "sugar-free." In response to ecology-minded consumers (and rising gas prices) car manufacturers are designing electric and hybrid automobiles in contrast to gas-guzzling SUVs. BP is producing and promoting alternative fuels. Realizing they could lose valuable brains to materity leave, spousal relocations, or other personal issues, companies created virtual officing.

It seems a function of human nature to create special words around the things we value. Whether those things are career, family, or products and services, they resonate more vibrantly when given their own vocabulary. What are the words that define your company or yourself? What words resonate internally or with consumers? What words help define who you are or what you want to become? For fifty years a mantra originally written for Cadillac in the 1930s—"On Excellence"—has been passed on to hundreds of companies. Occupations have their own terms of art. Lovers, families, and friends have their own special words, phrases, jokes that help to bind them together. Sacred words can also originate from a visionary leader.

Sometimes sacred words just happen. No one could have predicted the success of Verizon's "Can you hear me now?" query. Or Budweiser's old "Wassup?" campaign. The success of both were functions of execution, performance, and excellent luck.

Usually, sacred words are the domain of the wordsmiths whose occupation it is to create them. The copywriters, speechwriters, product managers, name labs, scriptwriters, and others who smash words together until they sparkle with attention-drawing originality.

Look at your products. Products like the iPod, grande latte, Big Mac, and Beemers hold a special reverence in our word set.

Look at your usage and processes. Downloading is an

invented sacred word. So are macrobiotic, on-demand and boot camp.

Look at your ways of doing business. E-business, synchronized commerce, and aromatherapeutic were all minted coinage for their respective enterprises.

Listen to your leaders. The words of Tom Watson, Jr., and Leo Burnett still resonate at their companies, although they have been dead for years. The National Geographic Society still operates from a sentence that cofounder Alexander Graham Bell wrote a century ago declaring that it should discover "the world and all that's in it". The philosophies, speeches, and remarks of Bill Gates, Jeff Bezos, Jack Welch, and Steve Jobs all resonate inside and outside their organizations.

Finally, you must find leaders. The natural place to look within large organizations is to the founder, chief executive officer, or president. Most of the leaders we see on the front covers of *Fortune* and *Forbes* have natural sizzle. People like Richard Branson, Jack Welch, Martha Stewart, and others are charismatic men and women who want to propel their ideas forward. Define who your leaders are. Is it the founder? The chief executive officer? The project or team leader? Is it you?

Volumes already have been written on leadership. The unique qualities and value of leaders do not need to be repeated here. Every company has their own criteria for who are the best leaders within their organization. Leaders declare the mission and set the vision. Leaders lead. People with those abilities need to be sought out at every level within the organization, whether they are the CEO, the project leader, design team leader, floor manager, or supervisor on the manufacturing floor. They must be capable of carrying through the mission and values of the organization and reinforce and reengage the people who belong.

In primal branding workshops we pass out a Coke bottle, a toy VW, a Lego brick, and other products. Then we ask people to fill in the creation story, rituals, pagans, and so forth for these well-known and established brands. To other groups, we pass out pictures of a fox, a campfire, and a kite and ask them to create a brand. People are remarkably clever when it comes to designing their own product from scratch (sometimes the people with the most imaginative ideas come from outside the marketing department).

Primal branding is about implementing all seven pieces of code. When marketers put their iconic logo on packaging, at point-of-purchase, on shopping bags, on billboards, on the Teletron screen, behind the players at tennis matches and baseball, basketball, and hockey games, and on subway cars, Nascar race cars, and hot-air balloons, this willy-nilly wallpapering of corporate logos wherever they can find a surface is not done so much in error as in frustration. As they face themselves in the mirror each morning marketers recognize that something is missing. But like Mr. Jones in the famous Dylan song, they don't know what it is. For them, branding is an intangible, an ether.

Now managers can audit their brand according to the primal branding construct and analyze where pieces of code exist and where they do not. They can manage the marketing communications mix by deciding where the seven pieces of code can be woven into the Internet, public relations, direct marketing, consumer advertising, B2B, customer relationship management, out-of-home media, product design, package design, and in-house communications.

Brands need to be updated periodically to excite and engage their audience again. Remember that Campbell's soup (discussed earlier) and car skins are continually refreshed. This rule of thumb is not just true for automobiles and packaged goods. All belief systems need to be reenergized lest they grow stale and risk public refusal.

Creating a corporate work culture that people can believe in is critical for employee enthusiasm, work performance, and efficiency. It also motivates vendors, suppliers, lenders, and others who come into contact with the organization. Establishing and promoting a working culture is critical when companies merge together. It is the clash of dissimilar cultures within merging organizations that creates confusion, disgruntled employees, and apathy. Culture creation is also critical for new companies. How rituals, icons, and other aspects are established within the workplace becomes the foundation for the company's future—and its success.

Understanding and managing the functions of primal branding helps C-suite executives (from CEO to COO) lead the culture-building process and willingly create crucial tangents with their staff and coworkers to build greater efficiencies, vision, employee spirit, and mission-critical coherence.

Consider also Corporation A and Corporation B who have merged to become Corporation AB. Once merged, AB develops a new creed or reason for being. New icons are created in the form of a new logo and a new sign on top of the building, and everyone gets new business cards. That's where most corporate reconfigurations end, and management breathes a sigh of relief. Coworkers are given the mandate, "now go, make, do." Meanwhile, the guy in the cube next to you has been transferred to Houston and the person on the other side has been right-sized. Recruiters march through their Rolodexes and cherry-pick the best managers and research scientists. As the new corporate entity unfolds, employees become dispirited. The job may be the same, but everything else is different. People begin to drift away, saying, "It's just not the same here anymore." Corporate management shrugs. Change is rough. Besides, this collateral damage happens during every merger, some people can't handle it, it's the cost of doing business.

Or consider the company in a growth spurt. New employees are arriving faster than bees to a honey jar. The company rapidly finds itself facing a crisis of spirit. The original employees complain that the new people "don't understand how we do things." Worse, because the new employees don't understand the values and mission of the company, they are importing their own. (In other words, polluting the company with the values and creeds and rituals of the companies they came from.) The result is a confused sense of mission, blurred motivations, loss of leadership, disgruntled employees, and apathy.

Using the principles of primal coding, however, leadership can manage the intangibles of their organization and willingly create, sustain, and motivate a new corporate culture concurrent with merger and new growth processes. Using primal branding, leaders can create and sustain a company and mission that people believe in. As the process evolves, managers find that they have people who feel they belong to the new organization. The essence of this belonging resonates in a refreshed sense of commitment, trust, empathy, vision, mission, and values within the organization. Instead of creating confusion, bewilderment, and fear, the primal code offers the potential to create an even stronger organizational culture than existed before.

Building corporate cultures is one of the most vital tasks facing organizations today. "Having a culture at RollerBlade was extremely important to our initial success," says former Rollerblade CEO John Sundet. "It was the glue that held things together. It was almost as important as innovation and product development."

"We started in a garage filled with office cubes," says Rand Miller, cofounder of Cyan Worlds. "We grew from there. But, actually, some of the same habits and spirit of Cyan were founded in that garage and continue today."

7. The Bones

Brands are ideologies with their own universe of truths, iconography, history, heroes, and demons. The power of a belief system is that it inherently contains relevance, vision, trust, empathy, leadership, vibrancy, resonance, and commitment, the very attributes companies spend millions of dollars each year trying to obtain.

Between exemplary examples like Nike and also-ran products like Lestoil lay thousands of companies in between. These are brands that have recognizable icons, fulfilling rituals, and enriched creation stories, but that lack other parts of the primal construct and are vulnerable to attack from more compelling brands.

While products and services need a functional reason for being, they also need its emotional counterpart in order to manifest their potential. It can be argued that Burger King has never been able to surpass McDonald's because McDonald's has more pieces of primal code in place. While BK has occasionally outperformed rivals in taste trials and promotional end runs, they have not been able to achieve the intangible visceral emotional connections—and hence preference —that McDonald's continually enjoys. (As a consumer I have vague knowledge that McDonald's was started by Ray

Kroc but am unaware of parallel creation stories for BK—just one important piece of code.)

Many products and services may have some primal code but leave their public tacitly desiring more. When they are all in place, people believe strongly. If just a few pieces of code are apparent, their belief is not as strong. An example. Many people know the basic story behind Verizon, a telephone company formed when GTE and Bell Atlantic merged. And Verizon's "Can you hear me now?" mantra from their wireless division has become popular parlance. After a few thousand impressions in newspapers, television, and other media, Verizon's red check mark also has been imprinted on us. Just knowing the creation story, icon, and sacred words of one stand-alone division we have a better overall feel for Verizon than we do for MCI, the ever anonymous AT&T, or newcomers Orange and Cingular.

But what about the rest of the primal code? Verizon would be well served if they broadened the scope of their marketing efforts across the rest. And they could deepen their success by doing the same for other business segments. To decline this opportunity means lost brand capital, lost opportunity, and lost potential revenues for investors, managers, employees, and shareholders.

Vibrant brands are alive and juicy with primal code; they make your nerve endings tingle. Brands devoid of code are stale, irrelevant, and flaccid.

Primal branding is an organizing principle that helps manage the intangibles of your organization. It defines a world that naturally organizes itself. Why do we try to organize the world? "So that we can navigate it," replies Richard

Saul Wurman. For two years or more, I have been sharing the primal construct with company presidents, CEOs, and senior managers around the country. Many have asked thoughtful, provocative questions that have caused me to think deeply about primal branding and its effects.

A well-meaning company president once said to me, "My clients don't care if I have icons or rituals." They don't care if you have an accounting department, either, but your business couldn't run without it. Brands cannot have visceral appeal without the primal code. The primal code is imbedded infrastructure; it is the bones of your organization. Like having an inventory system or a good health care plan, it simply helps the organization function better. Another person pointed out during a presentation, "I don't think anyone who goes to Starbucks knows anything about [Starbucks founder and CEO] Howard Schultz." The point is that the pieces of code are in place and help underpin the experience and define the brand. The more pieces of code communicated to your public, the stronger your cause, organization, product, service, or community. (While people may not be able to name Howard Schultz, strong leadership emanates from Starbucks, succinctly evidenced by their well-orchestrated experience.)

Creating a world of believers means creating a group of people who feel they belong to your ideals and want to convince others of your cause. People who wear Nikes instead of Adidas, drink Starbucks rather than Maxwell House, prefer Disney World over Universal and California wine over French will advocate their causes without blinking. Recall your first trip to Starbucks, your first trip to the grocery store or school in a new area where you relocated. Odds are, it was recommended to you by someone else. Advocates will tell you the why, what, who, and where without even being asked. This is what is commonly known as "word of mouth," the most potent and sought after form of delivering a brand message. The third-party endorsement of people who already belong to your brand, your belief, your cause is the strongest argument for persuading others. Their anecdotal personal histories persuade better than the millions of dollars funneled into promotional partnerships, Web sites, magazine campaigns, out-of-home, radio advertising, stunts, and other devices designed to stun, divert, bushwhack, and beguile us on the sponsor's behalf.

You don't ride a bike forty miles an hour down a steep dirt road because you got that bike for fifty dollars less than the guy riding behind you. You ride that bike for self-fulfillment, for the adrenalin rush, because the fat guy living next door to you can't or won't or is afraid to; you ride for affirmation, to defy death; you ride to scare your mother; you ride for a sense of love or abandonment or companionship; you ride because you need the endorphins; you ride because you are a screaming kamikaze who needs to feel the rattle of the road in your bones in order to feel like your life has meaning and substance and emotions that can't be expressed sitting behind a desk or basking in the communal fire of prime-time television. And sometimes you just ride the bike to get exercise.

Primal branding demonstrates how you can create passion for product and organization alike. It not only explains how phenomena occur, it shows how you can create them yourself. Think of the things that mean something to you.

They all come from someplace ("creation story"). They stand for something ("creed"). They are symbolized by a sign, a sound, a smell ("icon"). You do certain specified things regarding them ("rituals"). Certain words evoke that experience ("sacred words"). You contrast that experience against other experiences ("pagans"). They have an individual, whether real or fictional, who is behind the whole thing ("leader"). It's all about creating a sense of meaning. The resonance inherent in a brand subsumes the competition. When people believe in and belong to a brand experience it's no longer about the task, it's about the experience. When people shop for outdoor equipment they don't say, "We went shopping for a tent today." They say, "We went to REI." When people go for a cup of coffee, they say, "Let's go to Starbucks." When they travel out of state to gamble, they don't just say, "We went gambling." They say, "We went to Vegas." When they shop for laundry detergent and paper towels they say, "We went to Target."

There is a unifying principle today behind economics. There is a unifying principle behind physics. There is a unifying principle behind psychiatry. At the risk of inviting invidious comparisons, I suggest that primal branding is a unifying principle that helps manage the intangible, emotional pieces of your brand.

In today's results-driven-by-the-nanosecond economy CEOs and managers don't have time to fail. Chief executive officers have mandates to turn companies around, grow business, and benefit shareholders. Product managers have about eighteen months to make their mark. The cost of listing products at major retailers can be hundreds of thousands of dollars. This combination of less time and higher costs means there is little time for marketers to gain resonance and meaning. In this context, the primal code becomes invaluable as a central operating principle to give marketers the elements they need to help products resonate quickly and assume preferential status.

Because primal branding relates to people at a deep-skin, innately human level it transcends demographic and psychological borders and relates to people living in New York as readily as Bombay or São Paolo. The icons, rituals, sacred words, et al., will differ in order to fit into different ethnographic groups, but the essential primal concept is cross-cultural. The importance of this is clear as companies become more global, try to become relevant in differing cultures, try to speak to young people, and want consumer groups from Toronto to Timbuktu to feel they belong to their brand.

As we look at our society today the implications of the primal code not only influence our perception of products and services, it influences how we respond to social and political change. Look deeper into the wallpaper of our daily life and you see that the popular and deep-seated cultural changes are glistening with primal code. Others try to seize our attention, but without primal coding they fade and go dark.

Primal branding provides a lens through which you can guide marketing communications and influence suppliers, vendors, and financial advocates. It is a tool to help guide the way you hire and train employees and create new products and services, and the way that you embrace your consumers.

Primal branding also provides training managers and human resources staff with a system for integrating the spirit of the corporate body into new hires and other personnel. As a way of conveying the spirit of the enterprise, for example, instead of simply handing new hires their I.D. security card and benefits folder, HR can brief the new hire on the company's creation story and the creed, and begin the process of immersing them into your corporate culture.

There are patterns in the swirl of existence that seem nonexistent or incoherent until they finally reveal themselves. Alphabets, tectonic plates, streets, constellations, prime numbers, binary code, genetic strands: Once these patterns are explained and revealed we cannot look at the world in the same way again. Suddenly, we see the pattern, almost as if it were watching us all the time, wondering when we were going to discover it. The primal code is one such pattern.

Primal branding contains a web of relationships and inferences that bang at the drum of our emotional mind-set. It offers an irresistible concentration of meaning and a clarified way of perceiving brands. In the end, as we've seen throughout this book, it's not about price points, end-cap displays, demographic targets, or product innovation. It's about people. Sun-tanned, freckle-faced, buck-toothed human beings who orbit around a sun that glows with feel-good emotion, spontaneous gratification, and universal desire. What the primal code reveals is a new selling proposition that both appeals to and satisfies something elemental and inarticulate within humankind. We are like the bird that spots glittering foil and flies toward it. From the mass of choices available to us, from the thousands of items hollering for our attention, we walk away with whatever sparkles with primal code. The pattern of the primal code is palpable and powerful. It is felt by billions of people each day who are consumers, citizens, and converts inexorably drawn to products, civic causes, and communities of people that, glittering with primal code, they feel they belong to.

In closing, when people believe in something, they seek out others who believe in the same thing. These people can belong to a group of people who buy the same brand of coffee each morning or put on the same kind of shoes. They can be people who drive the same kind of car to work in the morning, or work in the same company, or live in the same city. They can be people who vote for the same political party, or who attend the same after-hours bullshit session, or watch the same sports events, or like the same music group, or play the same action game on the Internet. They call themselves enthusiasts, derived from the Greek word *enthusiasmos,* a state likened to being "filled with the gods." They call themselves fans, the short form for fanatics. They can be baseball nuts or skateboard freaks. Their most curious aspect is their extremism, their zeal. And it doesn't much matter if they are crazy about the coffee they drink or wild about their favorite car or human rights or saving the world. These people are committed.

They find each other in chat rooms, in clubs, groups, organizations, associations, unions, shopping clubs, political parties, societies, towns, and states. If their number is large enough they become a sect, a culture, a nation. The important factor is that they belong, and however you define their enthusiasm, evangelism, and zealotry, it sparks others to belong.

As marketers focus on increasing brand awareness, brand resonance, new product news, and brand personality through advertising and other brand marks they often (in fact, almost always) miss the opportunity to provide meaning and substance behind their products and services.

Throughout this book, I have outlined the seven attributes that make up the primal code, the spine of every belief system. These attributes are fundamental, rooted deep within the essence of humankind. As human beings, we want to believe, we must believe. Loss of faith is one of the great dramatic themes and one of mankind's most desperate acts. It is the despair of Willie Loman and King Lear. A look at human history reveals that all great movements have used the primal code to serve their purposes. Others have failed, either because they did not use the code wisely or did not use it at all. Primal branding has broken down the elements that help people feel better about a brand. This is not soft marketing. It is critical in today's parity marketplace when we can choose from over four hundred car styles, fifty kinds of toothpaste, and one hundred different soft drinks. Because when a customer is standing in the aisle, in the car dealership, or shopping on-line, when they simply feel better about Product X than Product Z; that is "preference." And it is axiomatic that increased preference leads to increased sales.

It comes down to perspective. Innovation, distribution, and lucky sales goals produce short-term gains. But if you are the owner, an investor, stockholder, or brand manager the goal is not just to seize short-term sales but also to create resonance and long-term value. The rigors of meeting day-to-day sales objectives may make the issue of *how customers feel* seem soft. But in today's parity world the soft sciences of human persuasion reveal some very hard business results. We cannot deny improved preference, increased brand value, better employee retention, greater job satisfaction, higher morale, the opportunities they imply.

Brands fail when they rely on functional attributes—bigger, faster, cheaper, more powerful, faster acting, or greater selection—and provide no deep-skin meaning. Brands fail when they prompt only a part of the system—they have a creation story, or pagans (usually a competitor), but leave the consumer waiting for the other pieces of primal code. When brands don't provide further plugs into the system the consumer never fully connects. The consumer (or audience, or political public) is left feeling unfulfilled and disappointed. Instead of becoming converts, they leave. Their departure might be instantaneous, or it may take years, but they vanish nonetheless. The result is lost revenue and lost opportunity for founders, employees, retailers, and shareholders.

No one doubts the value and power of brands. Marketers shrug wistfully when they are asked about the vibrancy of brands like Coke or Nike. They hit something big, they suggest, but nobody knows what it is, much less how to do it for their own products and services. Like the conference room meeting that started out this book, they point to the tried and true solutions everyone else attempts, the stuff that's hot at the moment. The fact is, brands that resonate not only fill coffers, they fulfill genuine pieces of the human psyche. As this book has illustrated again and again, the primal code is already the backbone for countless products and services, personalities and civic communities. They attach themselves to people in ways that are intangible and immutable. They are incomparable in ways that product benefits and solutions cannot resolve. They become the stuff of dreams.

In the end, the question that primal branding finally asks is, do you want to be just another bland service organization or product on the shelf, or do you want to become a necessary and desired part of the culture? As Maureen White, a former vice president at Target, said to me, "I get it. Don't just build a church; create a religion."

Acknowledgments

New ideas require ceaseless support and nurturing. Many people have helped support my thoughts since I first came up with the notions that ultimately became primal branding. Thanks to Tom Christopher, Brian Shepherd, Dick Staub, Wayne Gibson, Nadine Corrigan, Patricia Garcia-Gomez, and Christian Korbes for being the first line. Thanks to Robyn Waters, Scott Lutz, Michael Delgado, Bill Flanagan, Sarah Osmer, Larry Wu, Michael Houston, Marion Davidson, Karl Kalcher, Mary Horwath, Robin Steele, Betty Schweizer, and Anne Berg for mindfully listening and offering their professional eyes. Thanks to Pat Fallon, Richard W. Lewis, Doug Knopper, Nancy McNally, Tom Nelson and Steve Gardner, Claire Tondreau, Peter Engel, Steve Washburn, Robyn Anderson, and Maureen White for their support. Thanks, Paul. Thanks to the hundreds of people all across the country who patiently listened to my first-draft speeches on primal branding.

Thanks to Northrup Frye and Roland Barthes for being on the planet.

Thanks to my agent, Jonathon Lazear, for seeing and supporting what others did not. Thanks to my editor, Fred Hills, for his penetrating mind, as well as for being knowledgeable and patient. And to Nancy Jacobs, Terri Whitesel, Steve Holmes, Lisetta Koe, Sarah Pyle, Josh Staub, Stella Wilson, Alina Roberts, Leslie Kolleda, Robin Wark, Katie Garber, Chris Arnold, Rebecca Selva, Lisa Barrow, Cathleen A. Toomey, Duane Bates, M. J. Jacobsen, Beth Carmichael, and Terry Fassburg, without whose support far less would have been possible. Thanks to Dean Odegaard.

Thanks to all my girls—Erin, Kelly, Devin, Emma, Abigail—and the book club just for being so cute. And to my wife, Jane, whose wisdom and beauty are always inspirational.

And finally, thanks to David Altshul, who, after I explained the primal branding construct to him and acknowledged how hard it was to communicate to others, sagely replied, "The reason it's difficult to talk about is that you have something original to say." Thank you, David.

Bibliography

Dickinson, Emily. *The Complete Poems of Emily Dickinson,* edited by Thomas H. Johnson. Boston: Little, Brown, 1997.

Keegan, John. *The Iraq War.* New York: Knopf, 2004, p. 134.

Fast Company, July 2004.

Oprah Winfrey's Commencement Address, Wellesley College, May 30, 1997.

http://www.nationalgeographic.com/research/anthropology.html

http://www.vegas.com/index1.html;jsessionid=ce30a3b58e05$3F$D3 $9? key=home01

http://users.rcn.com/jkimball.ma.ultranet /BiologyPages/T/Taste.html

http://www.wellesley.edu/PublicAffairs/PAhomepage/winfrey.html

http://musicthing.blogspot.com/2005/05/tiny-music-makers-pt-1 -intel-inside.html

Index

Aardman Animations, 49
ABC, 164
Abley, Mark, 73–75
Absolut, 5, 23, 26, 27, 50–51
Accenture, 131
Achievement, icons of, 51
Acra, Reem, 33–34
Adcult USA (Twitchell), 209
Adidas, 100, 235
Advocate Lutheran General Children's
    Hospital, 61
Advocates, 235–36
Aeon Flux, 40
African Americans, 17
Agriculture, U.S. Department of, 143
AIDS, 9, 11, 35–36
Air Force, U.S., 139
Alinsangan, Susan, 51
Ally McBeal (TV show), 83
Altria Group, 19, 217
Altshul, David, 47–48, 50, 222
amazon.com, 11, 105, 219
American Historic Inns, 168
Andersen Consulting, 102
Andretti, Mario, 50
Angel Network, 193
AOL Time Warner, 19; Instant Messenger, 75
Apple Computer, 4, 8, 21, 26, 39, 74, 104,
    190–91, 218; creation story of, 11; iPod,
    27, 32, 51, 73, 76, 187, 191, 226; "Think
    different" campaign, 23, 71, 76–77
Applegate, Christina, 33
Ardente Winery, 179
Armani, 32
Armstrong, Lance, 36–37
Army, U.S., 139
Ashe and Spencer Music, 40
Askildsen, Tromod, 90
Atkin, Douglas, 209
Atkins diet, 106, 107

AT&T, 108, 234
Audi, 28–30
Audits, brand, 215, 228
Aveda Corporation, 23–24, 46–47, 67,
    146–53, 219; Shampure, 46, 148, 152
Averill, Steve, 187
A & W root beer, 41

Bank One, 107, 217
Barbie dolls, 32
Barkley, Charles, 23
Barnes & Noble, 24, 41
Bartles & James, 7, 217
Batman (movie), 190
Bauer, Alan, 59–60
Bauer, Eddie, 12
Beat Generation, 160
Beatles, the, 3, 14, 26, 32, 186
Beatrice Foods, 19
Bedbury, Scott, 209
Belief systems, 6–7, 9, 10, 99, 233, 240, 241;
    core principles of, 20; *see also* Ideologies
Bell, Alexander Graham, 227
Bell Atlantic, 234
Bellavia, Bianca Elise, 37
BellSouth, 5
Belonging, sense of, 7, 87–96, 99, 235, 240;
    of employees, 88, 93–94
Berry, Halle, 33
Berkeley, Linda, 220
Bernini, Gian Lorenzo, 223
Best Buy, 68, 210–11, 222
BET, 163
Bezos, Jeff, 11, 17, 105, 227
Bierut, Michael, 27, 36
Bill of Rights, 20
Bistro Don Giovanni, 180
Black-Eyed Peas, 205
BLK/MRKT, 204
Bloomenkranz, Larry, 125–30, 132, 133

Blue Man Group, 176
BMW, 53, 226
Bono, 187, 188, 192
Boots pharmacy chain, 82
Borders Book Stores, 41
Bowerman, Bill, 100
Brady Bunch, The, 11
Branson, Richard, 22, 26, 67, 78, 79, 227
Bridger, Jim, 178
British Petroleum (BP), 26, 225
Broadway on Broadway, 162–63
Broderbund, 109–10
Budweiser, 26, 40, 76, 226
Buehler Vineyards, 178
Built to Last (Collins), 209
Burger King, 40, 233–34; Whopper, 73
Burke, Jim, 83–85
Burnett, Leo, 37, 227
Business Week, 117
Butterfield, George, 80–81, 91–92
Butterfield, Martha, 91–92
Butterfield & Robinson, 63, 80, 91–93

Cakebread Cellars, 178, 181
California Raisins, 47
Campbell's soup, 12, 21, 211, 221, 229
Candler, Asa G., 102
Canyon Ranch, 63–64, 93–94
Capriati, Jennifer, 22
Carbohydrate Addicts, 107
Carlson, Chester, 17
Carlston, Doug, 109–10
Carson, Johnny, 185–86
Carson, Kit, 178
Carter, Jimmy, 35
Casey, Jim, 125–28, 133–34
Celebrities: as icons, 51; packaging of, 32–35; *see also* Personalities; *names of specific celebrities*
Chalone Wine Group, 177
Chamber of Commerce of the Future, 119
Chaplin, Charlie, 49
Character LLC, 47, 222
Charles, Ray, 176
Chateau Montelena, 177, 179
Chavez, Cesar, 78
Cherokees, 17
Chicago Cubs, 20
Chicken Run (movie), 49
China, Republic of, 13
Chipotle Mexican Grill, 42–44

Christmas icons, 31
Christo, 166
Chung, Peter, 40
Cingular, 234
Cinnabons, 26
Cirque du Soleil, 176
Citibank, 27
Clapton, Eric, 187
Clayton, Adam, 187
Clow, Lee, 51
Coastal Living magazine, 168
Coca-Cola, 4–5, 13, 41, 82, 199, 221, 242; bottle as icon for, 26, 27, 30, 228; creation story of, 11, 17; sacred words of, 101–2
Cold Stone Creamery, 54
Collins, Jim, 209
Company of Friends, 119
Community, sense of, *see* Belonging, sense of
Continental Congress, 136
Cooper, Sue Ellen, 87, 154–57
Corning Ware, 222
Costco, 30, 88
Council on Economic Priorities, 143
Countdown Entertainment, 163
Cowan, Benson, 92–93
Creation stories, 6, 9–20, 22, 30, 210, 216–18, 233–34, 237; destination, 160, 161, 166–67, 174, 177–78, 182; of history icons, 51; ideological, 105, 106; military, 136, 141; mythic quests in, 16–18; personality, 14–16, 185–87, 192–95, 198–200, 206; of product and service businesses, *see specific companies;* in team creation, 213; vision for future in, 18
Creeds, 6, 9, 19–25, 211, 215, 217–20, 237; destination, 161–63, 168, 171, 173–75, 178, 182–83; ideological, 105, 106; mergers and, 230; military, 135–37, 141; mission statements as, 20–21, 24–25; personality, 192, 195, 198, 201, 206; of product and service businesses, *see specific companies;* in team creation, 213; of victory icons, 51
Crocker, Betty, 12, 13, 27, 222
Cronkite, Walter, 198
Culting of Brands, The (Atkin), 209
Culture, corporate, 229–31, 238–39
Custer, Gen. George Armstrong, 37
Cyan Worlds, 79, 108–16, 231

Dale Air Limited, 44
Danone, 144, 145, 219–20

Darnell, Scott, 92
Darwin, Charles, 14
Davidson, Marshall, 137–41
Davis, Melinda, 209
Davis, Sammy, Jr., 176
Declaration of Independence, 20, 73
Dell, 102
Democratic Party, 162
Dempsey, Jack, 50
Destinations, 159–84, 209; icons of, 52; *see also* Irvington; Las Vegas; Napa Valley; Palm Jumeirah; Times Square
Dharma and Greg (TV show), 83
DHL, 132
Diageo LLC, 19; Captain Morgan's Rum, 18
Dickinson, Emily, 185
Dion, Celine, 176
Disney, Walt, 17, 22, 72, 78
Disney Corporation, 4, 5, 11, 12, 17, 22, 28, 161, 235
Durant, William C. "Billy," 18
Dvořák, Antonin, 199
Dykstra, Gretchen, 161–63, 165, 166

eBay, 27
Edison, Thomas, 11–12, 17, 22, 76, 78
Einstein, Albert, 76
Eisenstadt, Alfred, 160
Eisner, Michael, 22, 26, 78
Election (movie), 83
Elizabeth I, Queen of England, 32
Ells, Steve, 42–44
Eminem, 186
Employee behavior, 88, 212–13, 229–31, 238
Energizer batteries, 23
Ensign, Janet, 62
Environmental Protection Agency, 143
Eskew, Mike, 133
Estée Lauder, 146
Evans, Dave (The Edge), 187, 188, 191, 192
Express jeans, 205

Fairey, Shepard, 159, 199–206
Family Circle magazine, 193
Farber, Sam, 30
Fashions, iconic, 32–35
Fast Company magazine, 79, 116–24
FedEx, 11, 26, 73, 132, 219
Fender guitars, 31
Ferrari, 30
Fistful of Dollars, A (movie), 39

Flay, Bobby, 176
Forbes magazine, 117, 227
Ford, Henry, 17, 22
Ford Motor Company, 5, 13, 17, 18, 72; F-350 pickup truck, 22; Jaguar, 18, 22, 30
Fortune magazine, 117, 227
42nd Street Development Project, 161
Founders, 78; in creation stories, 11–13, 17; creed as legacy of, 22
French Laundry Restaurant, 180, 181
Frog's Leap Winery, 181
Full House (TV show), 83
FutureBrand, 129

Galligan, Tiffany, 36
Gandhi, Mohandas K., 13, 27, 76, 78
Gates, Bill, 22, 26, 78, 227
General Electric (GE), 11–12, 17, 22
General Mills, 18, 145, 222; Wheaties, 18, 32, 41; Hamburger Helper, 18
General Motors, 5, 18, 53, 221; Cadillac, 18, 31; Chevrolet, 18, 53, 72, 215; GMC, 215–16
Geographic locations, *see* Destinations
Gerstner, Louis W., 102, 103
Getty Center, 32
Gettysburg Address, 73
Gibson guitars, 31
Gilligan's Island (TV show), 11, 107
Ginsberg, Allen, 160
Giuliani, Rudolph, 160–61
Godin, Seth, 209
Goodrich tires, 4, 107
Goodyear, Charles, 17
Goodyear tires, 17
Google, 4, 9, 11, 20, 53, 57, 71, 90
Graves, Michael, 13
Great Britain, 13, 32
Green Giant, 27
Groth Vineyards & Winery, 178, 181
Guinness stout, 56
GTE, 234
Gula, Sharbat, 38
Gulf War, 139

Habitat for Humanity, 193
Hacker, Chris, 24, 46, 67, 147, 148, 150–52
Harpo Entertainment Group, 197
Harry Potter books, 45, 106
Hart, Melissa Joan, 33
Harvard Business Review, 116–18, 121–23
Hayden, Franz Joseph, 198

Heinz ketchup, 37–38
Hendrix, Jimi, 188
Hewson, Paul, *see* Bono
Hirshberg, Gary, 81–82, 142–46, 219–20
Hitchcock, Alfred, 39
Hollister Company, 74
Holmes, Steve, 130, 131
Holt, Douglas B., 209
Hope and Glory Inn (Irvington, VA),
   166–68, 170
How Brands Become Icons (Holt), 209
Howard Stern's Private Parts (movie), 83
HP, 67–68, 219
H & R Block, 5, 26
Hunt's ketchup, 37

IBM, 4, 5, 71, 74, 102–4, 131, 220; creation
   story of, 11, 18, 102; e-business of, 20,
   102, 104, 213; logo of, 27, 28
Icons, 6, 9, 10, 19, 26–52, 211, 216, 217, 220–23,
   234, 237; architectural, 41; aroma, 44–47;
   character, 47–50; destination, 159, 163–65,
   167–72, 175, 178–79, 183; ideological,
   105–6; mergers and, 230; military, 135,
   139, 141; personality, 187–88, 192, 194–96,
   198, 201, 206; of product and service
   businesses, *see specific companies*; socially
   significant, 35–37; sound, 39–41; taste,
   41–44; in team creation, 213; victory,
   51–52; visual, 27–39
Ideologies, 105–7
Ikea, 40
IMG, 22–23, 50
Imperial War Museum, 44
India, 13
Intel, 39; Pentium processor, 26
International Brotherhood of Teamsters, 130
Internet, 71, 105, 116, 123, 124, 155, 182, 240;
   as community, 95–96; creation stories
   on, 19; logging onto, 53; *see also* Google
Iran hostage crisis, 35
Iraq War, 136
Irish Americans, 17
Irvington (VA), 166–73, 183, 184
Isdell, E. Neville, 102
Italian Americans, 17–18
It Takes Two (movie), 83
Iwo Jima, battle of, 134–35

Jagger, Mick, 26, 192
Japan Society of New York, 116

Jaws (movie), 39
Jefferson, Thomas, 78, 136
Jeter, Derek, 22
Jobs, Steve, 11, 22, 26, 51, 76, 78, 190–91, 227
Johanson, Donald, 3
Johansson, Scarlett, 34
John, Elton, 176, 191
John Deere, 5, 28, 31
John Paul II, Pope, 95
Johnson, Betsy, 152
Johnson, Bryan, 65, 66
Johnston, Alastair, 22, 23, 50
Jordan, Michael, 14, 50, 100
Joseph, Jenny, 154, 156
Julia's Kitchen, 180

Kahlo, Frida, 27
Kaymen, Sam, 141–42, 145
Keegan, John, 136, 139
Keller, Thomas, 181
Kerouac, Jack, 160
Khrushchev, Nikita, 71
Kia, 107
Kidman, Nicole, 34
King, B. B., 187
King, Martin Luther, Jr., 27, 78
King of the Hill (TV show), 83
Kingpin (movie), 83
Kiss, 26, 186
Knight, Frank, 44–45
Knight, Phil, 78, 100
Komenda, Erwin, 28, 29
Korean War, 139
Kraemer, Tom, 51
Krispy Kreme, 41
Kristiansen, Gottfried, 57
Kristiansen, Ole Kirk, 56–57
Kroc, Ray, 233–34
Kudrow, Lisa, 33

Lagasse, Emeril, 176
Lance Armstrong Foundation (LAF), 36–37
Landor, 26, 88, 221
Language, *see* Sacred words
Las Vegas, 173–77, 184, 237
Leaders, 6, 9, 19, 78–85, 108, 227–28, 237;
   corporate culture and, 230–31;
   destination, 165, 177, 181; ideological,
   106, 107; military, 140; personality, 197,
   206; of product and service businesses,
   see specific companies

League of American Theaters, 161
Legally Blonde (movie), 129
LEGO, 5, 56–59, 89–91, 95, 228
Leighton, Fred, 34–35
Leno, Jay, 186, 198
Leonardo da Vinci, 31
Lestoil, 4, 107, 233
Letterman, David, 164, 185, 186, 193, 198
Lévi-Strauss, Claude, 54
Liberia, 17
Life magazine, 135
Lindberg, Chuck, 136
Liszt, Franz, 199
Logos, 12, 27–28, 99, 100, 105, 108, 187–88,
    211, 230
Lohan, Lindsay, 185
Lopez, Jennifer, 33, 35
Lovemarks (Roberts), 209
Lowery, Lou, 135
Luce, Henry, 22

Madonna, 11, 27, 66, 186
Mail Boxes, Etc., 129
Maktoum, Sheikh Mohammed bin Rashid
    Al, 181, 183
Mandela, Nelson, 17, 27, 78
Mantle, Mickey, 50
Marine Corps, U.S., 25, 134–41, 214
Mariott Corporation, 161
Marketing Evaluations, 195–96
Marlboro Man, 39
Marmaropoulos, George, 61–63
Martha Stewart Living Omnimedia, 194
Martin, Steve, 186
Martin guitars, 31
Maslow, Abraham, 7
Mass ideologies, 105–6
Matravers, Peter, 46, 47, 148–50, 153
Matthews, Dave, 13
Mays, Jay, 28
McCartney, Paul, 186
McCormack, Mark H., 23
McDonald's, 13, 26, 27, 41, 42, 233–34;
    Big Mac, 73, 226
McEnroe, John, 22–23
McGuinness, Paul, 187–93
MCI, 4, 107, 234
McIntyre-Velky, Catherine, 64
McKee, Jake, 89–91
McMullen, Larry, 187
Meier, Richard, 32, 223

Mercedes Benz, 53
Mergers, 217, 229–30
Metropolitan Opera, 39
Michelangelo, 31
Michelin tires, 27
Micron Technology, Inc., 107
Microsoft, 102
Miller, Mark, 176
Miller, Rand, 79–80, 109–19, 231
Miller, Ryan, 109, 110, 113, 115
Miller Brewing, 82
Mini Cooper, 4, 31, 187, 213
Miramounte Restaurant, 180
Mission Impossible (movie), 190
Mission statements, 20–21, 24–25
Mr. Clean, 27
M & Ms, 47–48
Mondavi Wines, 178
Monster's Ball (movie), 40
Montblanc pens, 5
Moore, Michael, 198
Morris, Errol, 12
Mother advertising agency, 82–83
Motorola, 220
Mozart, Wolfgang Amadeus, 198–99
MTV, 40, 163
Murphy, David, 69–70
Music, iconic, 39–41, 106
Mustards Grill, 180

Nader, Ralph, 122
Nakheel, 182, 183
Nantucket Nectars, 217
Napa Valley, 177–81
Nascar, 4, 14, 106, 228
National Geographic, 38, 220, 227
Nations, creation stories of, 13–14, 17
Native Americans, 17
Natural History Museum (London),
    44–45
Navratilova, Martina, 22
Navy, U.S., 139
NBC, 163
Nelson, Susan, 26, 88, 221
New Brand World (Bedbury), 209
New Culture of Desire, The (Davis), 209
New York Jets, 27
New York Times, The, 12, 160
Newman, Paul, 193
Newton, Wayne, 175, 176
Nicklaus, Jack, 22, 50

Nike, 4, 8, 9, 64, 74, 184, 224, 233, 235, 242; creation story of, 100; creed of, 21; Lance Armstrong Foundation wrist bands and, 36, 37; music for, 40; sports celebrities associated with, 48, 50, 100; swoosh icon for, 26, 48
Nonbelievers, *see* Pagans

Ogilvy, David, 22
Ogilvy advertising agency, 104
Oprah's Book Club, 193
Opus One, 24–25, 178–81
Oracle, 102
Orange cellular, 82, 234
Oreos, 41
Origins, *see* Creation stories
Orlando, Tony, 35
Osbourne, Ozzie, 13
OXO Good Grips, 30–31, 89

Packaging, iconic, 32–35, 37–38
Pagans, 6, 9, 19, 70–72, 225–26, 237; destination, 165, 173, 176, 180, 183; ideological, 106; military, 139, 141; personality, 192, 194, 197; of product and service businesses, *see specific companies*; team creation and, 214; victory icon, 51–52
Palmer, Arnold, 23, 50
Palmisano, Sam, 78, 103
Palm Jumeirah, 181–83
Parker, Sarah Jessica, 34
Patton (movie), 116
Pavlov, Ivan, 46
Payne, Alexander, 83
Pearson, David, 24–25, 179–80
Pei, I. M., 103
Pemberton, John, 11, 17, 101, 102
Penn, Sean, 66
Penn & Teller, 176
Pentagram Design, 27, 36
People magazine, 130, 185
Pepsi, 102
Permission Marketing (Godin), 209
Personalities, 185–204, 209; *see also* Fairey, Shepard; Stewart, Martha; U2; Winfrey, Oprah
Peters, Tom, 123
Petty, Richard, 14
Phelps, Joseph, 181
Phenomenology, 199–200, 205

Philips Medical Systems, 61–63
Pledge of Allegiance, 20
PlumpJack Winery, 181
Pollack, Sidney, 21
Pop ideologies, 106–7
Porsche, 29, 30
Portman, Natalie, 34
Post-it Notes, 27
Practice, The (TV show), 83
Pratt, Carl, 64, 93–94
Preference, 7
President's Council on Sustainable Development, 143
Presley, Elvis, 14, 27, 174, 175, 186, 188
Primal Digs, 210, 212–13
Prince, 186
Procter and Gamble, 18, 221; Tide, 12, 18, 26, 27
Products, 209, 233, 234, 238; *see also specific products and companies*
Progressive Insurance, 59–61
Protein Power, 107
Psycho (movie), 39
Puck, Wolfgang, 176
Pullman Palace Car Company, 128
Puma, 100
Pyrex, 222

Q scores, 196, 198
Queen, 13
Qwest, 107

Raleigh, Walter, 32
Ralenkotter, Rossi, 174, 176, 177
Rat Pack, 174
Rechelbacher, Horst M., 23–24, 146–47
Red Bull, 205
Red Cross, 26
Red Hat Society, 87, 154–57
Red Wing Shoe Company, 12, 69–70
Reese, Tom, 161
REI, 54, 237
Renew America, 143
Rheingold, Howard, 95–96
Rhode Island School of Design, 199
Richards, Keith, 26, 193
Riggio, Len, 24
Riney, Hal, 7
Rio Grande (movie), 39
Rituals, 6, 9, 10, 19, 52–70, 210–11, 217, 223–25, 237; of daily life, 52–53;

destination, 162–64, 169, 172–73, 175–76, 179–80; engineering positive, 56–70; ideological, 105–7; military, 137–39; personality, 188–89, 192, 194, 196, 198, 201–4, 206; of product and service businesses, *see specific companies;* team creation and, 213; victory icon, 51; workplace, 54–55
Roberts, Kevin, 209
Robinson, Sidney, 91–92
RollerBlade, 231
Rolling Stone, 118, 188
Rolling Stones, 26, 187
Romantic Homes magazine, 154
Rose, Charlie, 185
Rosenthal, Joe, 135
Rural Education Center, 142
Rysher Entertainment, 83

Sacred words, 6, 9, 19, 72–77, 226–27, 234, 237; creation of, 76–77; destination, 176–77, 180–81; ideological, 106, 107; military, 137, 139–41; personality, 192, 194, 196–98, 204, 206; of product and service businesses, *see specific companies*; team creation and, 213; of victory icons, 52
Sainsbury's, 68
Saint, The (movie), 83
St. Petersburg, University of, 46
Samsung, 210–11, 221
Sara Lee, 5
Saturn, 7, 53, 56, 219
Saved by the Bell (TV show), 83
Sawyer Cellars, 179
Schoenfeld, Gerry, 161
Schultz, Howard, 12, 100, 235
Schwartz, Sherwood, 11
Scott, George C., 116
Seal, 66
Seattle's Best Coffee, 5
Seinfeld (TV show), 73
Services, 209, 233, 234, 238; *see also specific companies*
7Up, 71
Shubert Organization, 161
Sideways (movie), 83, 179
Siegfried & Roy, 175
Silverado Vineyards, 178
Simpson, Ashley, 185
Simpson, Jessica, 14

Sinatra, Frank, 176, 188
Singapore Zoo, 25
Sloan Management Review, 122
Smart Design, 31, 67–68, 222
Smart Mobs (Rheingold), 95
Smirnoff, 210
Smith, Brendan Powell, 57
Smith, Jedediah, 178
Snaps licorice, 41
Snoop Dog, 186
Sopranos, The (TV show), 107
South Africa, 17
South Beach Diet, 106, 107
Soviet Union, 11, 17, 55
Spears, Britney, 14, 66
Spencer, Thad, 40
Spielberg, Stephen, 14
Spoken Here (Abley), 73
Spring Mountain Vineyard, 177
Springsteen, Bruce, 185
Sproxton, David, 49
Stag's Leap Wine Cellars, 177, 179, 181
Stalin, Joseph, 71
Starbucks, 4–5, 8, 53, 71, 99–100, 211, 235, 237; creation story of, 12, 99; mermaid icon of, 12, 26, 28, 221; sacred words of, 72, 74, 100; "third place" creed of, 25, 99, 219
Starck, Philippe, 13
Star Trek (TV show), 107
Steele, Robin, 40
Steinem, Gloria, 78
Stew Leonard's, 224
Stewart, Martha, 27, 56, 79, 159, 193–94, 222, 227
Stonyfield Farm, 81, 141–46, 219–20
Stowell, Davin, 31, 67–68, 89, 222
Strank, Mike, 135
Street, Picabo, 23
Studio Number One, 204
Styx, 13
Sugar Busters, 107
Sulzberger, Arthur, 161, 165
Sundet, John, 231
Sunkist, 105

Taco Bell, 42, 71
Tanimoto, Craig, 76
Tarantino, Quentin, 217–18
Target, 12–13, 26, 50–51, 211, 221, 222, 237, 243

Tatler-Cunard Travel Guide, 168
Taylor, Bill, 117, 118, 120, 122, 124
Taylor, Jim, 83
TBWA\Chiat\Day, 23, 51, 76
Tchaikovsky, Piotr Ilich, 199
Team creation, 213–14
TED Conferences, 77, 95
Teets, Robin, 37–38
Terra Restaurant, 180
Texas Instruments, 22
Thomas, Freeman, 28–30, 80
3M, 28
Thurman, Uma, 34
TIES, 216
Time, Inc., 22
Times Square, 159–66, 184
Tomb Raider (movie), 190
Tonight Show, 39
Tony the Tiger, 27, 48–49
Tour de France, 36, 37
Towers, Jeremiah, 42
Townsend, Peter, 188
Travel & Leisure magazine, 168
Truchard Vineyards, 179
Turner, Ted, 22, 78
Twitchell, James B., 209

Unilever, 5, 53
United Airlines, 27
United Nations, 218
United States of America, 11, 20, 88;
    creation story of, 17; icons for, 26, 39,
    106, 222
Universal Studios, 235
UPS, 5, 18, 23, 28, 125–34, 218–20
U2, 9, 187–93

Valentine, Robert, 193
Valentino, 35
Van Halen, 66
Verizon, 217, 226, 234
Vietnam War, 136
Vinton, Will, 47
Virgin, 18, 26; Air, 66–67
Virtual Community, The (Rheingold), 95
Volkswagen (VW), 27, 29, 51, 88, 228;
    Beetle, 28–30, 213

Volvo, 25, 219
Vongerichten, Jean-Georges, 176

Waite, Mark, 82–83
Wall Street Journal, The, 130
Wallace & Gromit (TV series), 49
Wal-Mart, 49, 68
Wang, Vera, 152
Warhol, Andy, 9, 11, 27, 221
Washington, George, 78, 106
Waters, Alice, 42
Waters, Robyn, 70–71
Watkins, Tom, 22
Watson, Tom, Jr., 78, 102, 103, 227
Webber, Alan, 116–24
Weddings (Stewart), 194
Weiden+Kennedy, 64
Weinstein, Harvey, 193
Welch, Jack, 26, 78, 227
Westbrook, Bill, 166–73, 184
Westbrook, Robert, 169–70, 172
White, Maureen, 243
Williams, Serena, 22
Willis, Bruce, 66
Winfrey, Oprah, 4, 9, 11, 27, 78, 79, 159,
    194–98
Witherspoon, Reese, 33
Wonder, Stevie, 27
Woodruff, Robert, 102
Woods, Tiger, 14, 22, 48, 50, 100, 159, 185
World, The, 183
World Poker Tour, 106
World War II, 134–35, 160, 174
World Wrestling Entertainment, 54
Wozniak, Steve, 11
Wurman, Richard Saul, 77, 234–35

Xcel Energy, 107, 108
Xerox, 17, 22

Yount, George de la Concepcion, 178

Z-Brand, 65–66
Zeta-Jones, Catherine, 35
Zionists, 17
Zone diet, 107
Zyman, Sergio, 102

About the Author

PATRICK HANLON has served as a senior executive at the world's most creative advertising agencies, working on famous brands including Absolut, UPS, Sears, and IBM. In August 2003, he founded Thinktopia and began sharing the primal branding concept with marketers at Target, Lego, Starbucks, and elsewhere. He lives in Minneapolis.